THE AGE
OF SCANDAL

An Excursion through a Minor Period

T. H. WHITE

With twelve plates

PENGUIN BOOKS
IN ASSOCIATION WITH
JONATHAN CAPE

Penguin Books Ltd, Harmondsworth, Middlesex
AUSTRALIA: Penguin Books Pty Ltd, 762 Whitehorse Road,
Mitcham, Victoria

—

First published by Jonathan Cape 1950
Published in Penguin Books 1962
Reprinted 1963

—

Copyright © T. H. White, 1950

—

Made and printed in Great Britain
by C. Nicholls & Company Ltd
Set in Monotype Baskerville

Quotations from the works of Lytton Strachey and G. M. Trevelyan
are made by kind permission of the authors or their representatives,
and of Messrs Chatto & Windus Ltd and
Longmans, Green & Co. Ltd.

Contents

'Clio is one of the most glorious of the Muses; but, as everyone knows, she (like her sister Melpomene) suffers from a sad defect: she is apt to be pompous. With her buskins, her robes, and her airs of importance she is at times, indeed, almost intolerable. But fortunately the Fates have provided a corrective. They have decreed that in her stately advances she should be accompanied by certain apish, impish creatures, who run round her tittering, pulling long noses, threatening to trip the good lady up, and even sometimes whisking to one side the corner of her drapery, and revealing her undergarments in a most indecorous manner. They are the diarists and letter-writers, the gossips and journalists of the past, the Pepyses and Horace Walpoles and Saint-Simons, whose function it is to reveal to us the littleness underlying great events and to remind us that history itself was once real life.'

LYTTON STRACHEY

CHAPTER ONE

The Age of Scandal

WELL, we have lived to see the end of civilization in England. I was once a gentleman myself. When I was an undergraduate at Cambridge, the Master of a college was a fabulous being, who lived in a Lodge of breathtaking beauty and incalculable antiquity, tended by housemaids, footmen, and a butler. There he consumed vintage port, wrote abstruse treatises if the spirit moved him, and lived the life of an impressive, cultivated gentleman. Such posts were among the few and noble rewards rightly offered to scholarship by the civilization which then existed.

When I last stayed in Cambridge, I lunched with two Masters of colleges. Both of them had to help with the washing-up after luncheon.

There was a comic story current shortly after the Hitler war – one tried to think that it was comic. It said that there was some conference or other at Lambeth, thronged with Archbishops, Cardinals, Patriarchs, Moderators, and so forth. The Archbishops of Canterbury and York were seen to be in earnest consultation in one corner of the room. Were they discussing a reunion with Rome or a revision of the Prayer Book? Thrilled with the ecclesiastical possibilities of such a meeting, one of the stripling curates managed to edge himself within earshot of these Princes of the Church. They were discussing whether it was worse to wash-up or to dry-up.

The Earl of Shrewsbury – the 21st and premier earl

of Great Britain – whose ancestors have served the crown, and thus the nation, in one way or another, for about 800 years, has become a 'barrow-boy'. He sells fruit in the open air at a stall by the roadside.

A deceased female Labour Minister has given an interview to an American journalist, after driving the Earl Marshal of England out of his own home. The family pictures have been sold, she said with glee, and I can assure you that the Duke of Norfolk will never again be able to live in this house. 'We had our revolution during the war. We did not cut off their heads, we only cut off their incomes.' Yet the family of the Duke of Norfolk had served the crown on the battlefield, in the cabinet, and in the precursor of Miss Bondfield's 'Civil Service', for many and many generations.

They were generations of statesmen and proconsuls, who gave their sons in war more lavishly than any other class. Yet we have lived to see a Labour Minister of War stating that he does not give a tinker's curse for people of that sort, and the Minister of Health describes them indiscriminately as 'vermin'.

It is useless to whine. It has happened. It is the logical result of our half-baked Victorian humanitarianism. All men are not equal. That ridiculous idea of English democracy was invented in the reign of Queen Victoria, and it has now become bureaucracy.

So, now that it is no longer possible to be a gentleman, now that there is no longer enough time or money to be cultured, now that civilization has vanished along with the Word which gentlemen once kept. Now that glorious palaces like Knoe, Stowe, Wentworth Woodhouse, Bodiam, Montacute, Stourhead, Polesden Lacey, Blenheim, and the rest of them, are, or are likely to be, 'nationalized' for the wonderful proletariat, while the owners who gave their ancestors to make them lovely crouch in a couple of rooms in one wing, I have been looking back along the corridors of history, taking stock of that venture which once brought England to the leadership of the world. I believe that the peak of British culture was reached in the latter years of George III: that the rot began to set in with the 'Romantics': that the apparent prosperity of Victoria's reign was autumnal, not vernal: and that now we are done for.

I have been consoling my old age by running away from the Bondfields and the Shinwells and the Bevans, by going back to the grand old days of Horace Walpole, and I have written this book in the effort to give one last, loving, and living picture of an aristocratic civilization which we shall never see again.

*

DR JOHNSON: Mason is a Whig, Sir.

MRS KNOWLES (not hearing quite distinctly): A prig, Sir, did you say?

JOHNSON: No, madam, a Whig, but he is that too.

The old rhinoceros was right, for the Rev. William Mason was a prig to the backbone; though he was a harmless one. But he did invent – or he did adapt from Middleton's *Cicero* – a new kind of biography which led to the greatest Life in the English language.

Before Mason, a biographer had been content to write about the subject in his own words. Mason invented the idea of letting the subject speak for himself. In his Life of Gray, he strung together a selection of the poet's letters – and sometimes even forged them – supplying the necessary links in a running commentary. Horace Walpole was delighted with it.

Were I to judge from my own feelings [he wrote] I should say there never was so entertaining or interesting a work:

that it is the most perfect model of biography; and must make Tacitus, and Agricola too, detest you.

Later, when Dr Johnson published a Life of the same poet, Horry was furious.

Somebody asked Johnson if he was not afraid that *you* would resent the freedoms he has taken with Gray, '*No, no, Sir; Mr Mason does not like rough handling*' . . . The saucy Caliban!

There was another contemporary who agreed with Walpole that this new kind of Life was a 'perfect model of biography', and who thought that, by adding conversations to the letters which he reported verbatim, the idea might be improved.

Instead of melting down my materials into one mass [wrote Boswell in the Introduction to his immortal work] and constantly speaking in my own person . . . I have resolved to adopt and enlarge upon the excellent plan of Mr Mason, in his Memoirs of Gray. Wherever narrative is necessary to explain, connect, and supply, I furnish it to the best of my abilities; but in the chronological series of Johnson's life, which I trace as distinctly as I can, year by year, I produce, wherever it is in my power, his own minutes, letters or conversation, being convinced that this mode is more lively, and will make my readers better acquainted with him . . . Indeed, I cannot conceive a more perfect mode of writing any man's life.

*

In this little scrap-book of a nostalgic Tory, I have tried to extend Mason's kind of biography to an Age, attempting rather to string together a series of quotations from the people themselves, than to speak 'in my own person' – 'by which', as Boswell added with self-sacrifice and some regret, 'I might have appeared to have more merit in the execution of the work'.

In short, I have here tried to picture the nature and history of a minor period in its own words rather than in mine.

People are inclined to write as if the Age of Reason continued until the Romantic Revival, or as if the Augustan period were an unbroken whole. But the eighteenth century was split by a remarkable line of cleavage.

In the first half of the century, the authors became rulers: in the second, the rulers became authors.

If we look at the authors and the rulers before 1750, the difference is striking. On the one hand stand the omnipotent Popes and Swifts, courted or bribed or feared by servile lords, whom they bullied with a will; on the other hand lie the wincing upper classes, who had to buy their peace of mind by preferments or by actual money payment, prostrate before the bitter ink. The wicked old Duchess of Marlborough in the first half had to pay Pope £1,000, now worth perhaps ten times that sum, to suppress a satire on herself. He took the money, but did not suppress the satire. Swift bullied the cabinet itself till they did not know whether they were on their heads or their heels. He made the Princess of Wales invite him nine times before he would call at her house.

That was in the true Age of Reason, when Goldsmith could complain that he had been slighted by a mere lord. 'I met him,' he said indignantly, 'at Lord Clare's in the country, and he took no more notice of me than if I had been an ordinary man.' 'A nobleman,' agreed the Johnson of that period, 'ought to have made up to such a man as Goldsmith, and I think it is much against Lord Camden that he neglected him.' It was thought 'foolish' of Pope to give his friendship to ordinary peers, although he always kindly assured them that he did not value them as such.

The writers, in fact, were then full and complex characters. We may still puzzle about the relationship between Stella and her gloomy Dean, still argue about his persecution mania, his crooked personality, and the diseases from which he suffered. Pope, with his bent body, stays, deceitful stratagems, and delusions of grandeur, is a person whom we would recognize if we met him now – where we should find some difficulty in distinguishing between Lords Marlborough and Chesterfield, except by the eyebrows of the latter.

In short, during the real Age of Reason, it was the Grub Street authors who were articulate, powerful, and able to stamp themselves on posterity as people. It was to them that the fluttering cabinet ministers had to act as toad-eaters, and it was the literary standard of culture, dictated from below, which dominated a largely illiterate peerage.

I must tell you [wrote Lord Chesterfield to his son in 1750], that orthography, in the true sense of the word, is so absolutely necessary for a man of letters, or a gentleman, that one false spelling may fix a ridicule upon him for the rest of his life. And I know a man of quality who never recovered the ridicule of having spelled *wholesome* without the *w*.

The last fifty years of the century were directly the reverse of this. It was then the fourth Earl of Orford (Horace Walpole) who terrified the leaders of Grub Street and who drove young poets to suicide: it was the kings and the lords who were remembered, not the scribbling commons. George II, suffering from piles, lecturing the royal family, or standing with his sword advanced like a fencing master, after his horse had run away with him at Dettingen: George III with his 'What, what?': the fat and rather touching Florizel (George IV): the garrulous Clarence (William IV): these were real people seen in the round. It was the upper classes who now held the stage with their articulacy, the Walpoles, Herveys, Selwyns, Hollands, Boswells, or even

Brummells. Literature had passed to the aristocracy, and the poets were disregarded people like the clergyman Mason, or like Blake, who was unknown, or like the rusticated Cowper with his pet hares. Towards the end of the new period, Moore was boasting that Sir Walter Scott had called him 'a truly *gentleman* poet', while the plebeian Wordsworth was 'too much of the poet'. Professional writers, by some strange fatality, had even begun to have ridiculous names, like Crabbe, Hogg, etc. By then the miserable bard was a lank, bony figure, with short black hair, who writhed and showed his teeth in a grin of earnestness while his verses were being criticized, exclaiming: 'Is that poetry, Sir? Is it Pindar?'

'Here is an error, Sir; you have made Genius feminine.' – 'Palpable, Sir,' cried the enthusiast; 'I knew it. But [in a lower tone] it was to pay a compliment to the Duchess of Devonshire, with which her Grace was pleased. She is walking across Coxheath, in the military uniform, and I suppose her to be the Genius of Britain!'

By 1780, Johnson himself, when flattered by Lord Newhaven, was bowing 'his head almost as low as the table, to a complimenting nobleman'.

Naturally the division between the two ages was not a hard and fast one. Life was inclined to proceed by stages, and there were exceptions to everything. There were many bridges between the two halves. Dr Johnson was such a bridge; he was the last of the great Moguls of Grub Street, who lived into the patrician period. In the same way, Horace Walpole was a bridge. He was perhaps the first of the great Moguls of aristocracy, born within the Age of Reason. They lay parallel. The last writer and the first lord bound the ranks together – as did Chesterfield, Hervey, and Lady Mary Wortley Montagu – but it remains true, none the less, that the century began with power to the writers, and ended with power to the lords. It was literary power.

The atmosphere of the second epoch was different from the Age of Reason's: so different that the period seems to require a label of its own. One might suggest, the Age of Scandal.

Between the Classical and the Romantic movements, as they are recognized at present, there existed this other age, which was one of peculiar flavour. It filled the hiatus between Pope and Wordsworth with a distinct and unique culture, none the less real because it is seldom recognized now. It could be roughly dated between the death of Pope and the publication of the Lyrical Ballads, except that such dates are confusing. Periods do not exist between fixed years. They have forerunners in the previous age and laggards in the subsequent one. Although the Age of Scandal was at its height in the seventeen-eighties, under its greatest product, Horace Walpole, yet, between forerunner and laggard, it may be said to have stretched from Lady Mary Wortley Montagu to Croker or to Creevey.

The people of the late eighteenth century and of the Regency were different from the Augustans. They were not cold and formal like a heroic couplet but, on the contrary, eccentric, individual, sentimental, dramatic, tearful, even doggy. For that matter, they were a good deal more 'romantic', in the exact sense of that term, than the unsmiling crocodile of Rydal. Their heiresses frequently ran away with the footmen.

Few people seem to realize how charming and peculiar the Age of Scandal was. We have to dismiss so much from our minds before we can crawl inside theirs: before we can picture the powdered gentlemen in silks and laces, with their jewellery and the swords which they were ready to draw, with their sedan chairs and lap dogs and immense bets and deep potations. One of the commonest words about male clothes, in the letters of the reprobate Duke of Queensberry, was 'pretty'. One of his presents to the Prince Regent was a muff. Among the commonest reactions from readers and playgoers was that of tears. They adored their dogs and sent them tender messages in their letters. They were emotional about their friends, catty about their enemies, unusual in their hobbies, and singular in themselves. They were perhaps the first people in English literature to be real enough for gossip.

Gossip must be about character. It is useless to gossip about an unknown character, impossible to tell a good story about a person without foibles; for it is the foible which gives the story point. These people had characters, were among the first people in England who were sufficiently peculiar, in a modern way, to be apprehended by us as personalities. They did extraordinary things: puffed and blew like Dr Johnson, or went to executions like the sinister Selwyn, or constructed the astonishing tower of Fonthill like Beckford, or said that they were about to give birth to the Messiah like Joanna Southcott – or to a litter of rabbits like Mary Tofts. They fought duels in balloons like M. le Pique in 1808 – the first human being ever to be shot down in aerial combat – or directed their farm labourers with a megaphone and a telescope like Sydney Smith in his 'rheumatic armour'. Sometimes they could never be sure whether they were men or women, like the Chevalier d'Éon, and sometimes they dislocated London's milk supply, as was the case with the fourth Duke of Queensberry – who was supposed to take his early bath in this liquid before it was retailed – with the consequence that for many years nobody in London felt secure about the morning tea.

The Age of Scandal was the reverse of being a pompous one. Gossip is not pompous. It was inevitably an age of intimacy and of nicknames. Creevey was a product of it, and, as Lytton Strachey has pointed out:

There are no great names in his vocabulary – only nicknames: George III is 'old Nobs', the Regent 'Prinney', Wellington 'the Beau', Lord John Russell 'Pie and Thimble', Brougham, with whom he was on very friendly terms, is sometimes 'Bruffam', sometimes 'Beelzebub', and sometimes 'Old Wickedshifts'; and Lord Durham, who once remarked that one could 'jog along on £40,000 a year', is 'King Jog'.

It was because these people were aristocrats. The gossips lived in a small society which scarcely touched the middle classes of Wesley, nor the peasantry, nor the Mob. Literature had for the first time since Elizabeth become the medium instead of the plaything of the gentry. They moved in the tight world of the Drawing-rooms and of the Birthdays, knew each other as well as the boys at a public school in England might know each other today, chatted about the latest scandal, and, because they had learned to be literate, they wrote it down. So they remain in literature, even in the days of Attlee, mainly in the literature of letters and memoirs, as individual and as well preserved as they were in life. They were as real as Pepys. There is nothing so false as to suppose that they were a tired remainder from the era of Pope, waiting for the revival of Wordsworth. They were far from being classically cold. Indeed, to the reader of the *Newgate Calendar* or of Walpole's news-of-the-day or of the *Gentleman's Magazine*, it sometimes seems that there can have been no period so *Elizabethan* in its drama and tragedy and eccentricity as the end of the so-called Age of Reason.

THE AGE OF SCANDAL

Perhaps no set of men and women [said Trevelyan] since
the world began enjoyed so many different sides of life,
with so much zest, as the English upper class at this period.

CHAPTER TWO

Agrémens

HORACE WALPOLE, says Cunningham, had 'seen in the flesh two heroines of De Grammont and the Restoration, La Belle Jennings and Arabella Churchill, and lived long enough to offer his coronet to two ladies (Mary and Agnes Berry) who lived far into the reign of Queen Victoria'.

So extensive a panorama, stretching from the diamond-hilted sword and ruffle to a group of top-hats standing round a railway train, cannot easily be treated as a whole, unless it is realized that the gap between swords and trains was really a narrow one. In an age whose men had carried muffs and whose women had worn head-dresses so high that they had to sit on low stools in their coaches, swords only began to go out of fashion in 1780, when umbrellas came in. (Umbrellas, indeed, were carried by officers during the battles of the Peninsular War, though Wellington was inclined to disapprove. 'The Guards may in uniform, when on duty at St James's, carry them if they please; but in the field it is not only ridiculous but unmilitary.') Gentlemen wore wigs or powder till about 1800 – Lord Bathurst, the Colonial Secretary, cut off his pigtail in 1828 and sent it round to his colleagues in an official box – while Creevey was inspecting a puffing billy, in a top-hat, in 1829. There was a collision between cultures at the turn of the century, a rapid acceleration, so that at Horace Walpole's death the old world of the Stuarts and of the Tudors suddenly, rather than gradually, gave way to

the new world of the Industrial Revolution. In less than
a generation, the male population shed their finery and
cosmetics for the eclipse plumage of modern times. The
change happened under the guidance of Beau Brummell, though Fox, according to Wraxall, had 'first
thrown a sort of discredit on dress' – and this great
alteration, which Walpole had seen to begin, took
place within the Age of Scandal. The date was about
1793.

His is consequently a difficult time to imagine; for
half its writers were dressed in velvet and brocade –
Lady Mary Wortley Montagu, Lord Hervey, and Walpole himself – while the other half, born well within
Walpole's lifetime – Creevey, Greville, or Croker – were
in morning coats and pantaloons. Its lengthy ascendancy stretched from the last efforts of the Stuarts to
regain the throne, through the Spanish and Austrian
wars, the campaigns of India and Canada, the Seven
Years War, the loss of America, the French Revolution
and the struggle with Napoleon, to the days of the
Reform Bill.

Perhaps three quotations about transport may serve
to stitch the period together.

In 1773, Dr Johnson, whose idea of bliss was 'driving
briskly in a post-chaise', gave Boswell a piece of information about the possible speeds of earlier days.

The English [said he] are the only people who ride hard
a-hunting. A Frenchman goes out upon a managed horse,
and capers in the field, and no more thinks of leaping a
hedge than of mounting a breach. Lord Powerscourt laid a
wager, in France, that he would ride a great many miles in
a certain short time. The French academicians set to work,
and calculated that, from the resistance of the air, it was
impossible. His lordship, however, performed it.

As late as 1784, de la Rochefoucauld was explaining,

with reference to English race-horses, that 'when you are close to them you can hardly follow them with the eye – they travel more swiftly than a flash of lightning. The jockeys are obliged to keep their heads low in order to breathe. Their passage through the air is so swift that otherwise they would be choked.'

In 1829, Creevey had a lark of a very high order.

Today we have had a *lark* of a very high order. Lady Wilton sent over yesterday from Knowsley to say that the Loco Motive machine was to be upon the railway at such a place at 12 o'clock for the Knowsley party to ride in if they liked, and inviting this house to be of the party. So of course we were at our post in three carriages and some horsemen at the hour appointed. I had the satisfaction, for I can't call it *pleasure*, of taking a trip of five miles in it, which we did in just a quarter of an hour – that is, twenty miles an hour. As accuracy upon this subject was my great object, I held my watch in my hand at starting, and all the time; and as it has a second hand, I knew I could not be deceived; and so it turned out that there was not the difference of a second between the coachee or conductor and myself. But observe, during these five miles, the machine was occasionally made to put itself out or *go it*; and then we went at the rate of 23 miles an hour, and just with the same ease as to motion or absence of friction as the other reduced pace. But the quickest motion is to me *frightful*: it is really flying, and it is impossible to divest yourself of the notion of instant death to all upon the least accident happening. It gave me a headache which has not left me yet. Sefton is convinced that some damnable thing must come of it.

Whether something damnable came of it or not, whether human happiness has advanced since those days or retrograded, it is true to say that the central king of Walpole's five, George III, had been ruling over an England which was at one of the peaks of her greatness.

It is only [wrote G. M. Trevelyan] in the years that followed (1740–80) that we find a generation of men wholly characteristic of the Eighteenth Century ethos, a society with a mental outlook of its own, self-poised, self-judged, and self-approved, freed from the disturbing passions of the past, and not yet troubled with anxieties about a very different future which was soon to be brought upon the scene by the Industrial and French Revolutions. The gods mercifully gave mankind this little moment of peace between the religious fanaticisms of the past and the fanaticisms of class and race that were speedily to arise and dominate time to come. In England it was an age of aristocracy and liberty of the rule of law and the absence of reform; of individual initiative and institutional decay; of Latitudinarianism above and Wesleyanism below; of the growth of humanitarian and philanthropic feeling and endeavour; of creative vigour in all the trades and arts that serve and adorn the life of man.

It was an England, however, in which some of the refinements were still at a primitive level. In Lady Mary Wortley Montagu's time, gentlemen had not been expected to shave daily. Washing had been performed in a hand-basin. Chamber-pots had been kept in the dining-room sideboard, for the use of those who sat after the ladies had retired. Instead of the water-closet, which was re-introduced at the end of the century, there was the *chaise percée*: sometimes in a separate room, as was the case when George II died upon the stool; sometimes only behind a curtain, as it was when Lord Hervey had a contretemps in 1742.

The late Lord Privy Seal has had a most ridiculous accident at Bath: he used to play in a little inner room; but one night some ladies had got it, and he was reduced to the public room; but being extremely absent and deep in politics, he walked through the little room to a convenience behind the curtain, from whence (still absent) he produced himself in a situation extremely diverting to the women; imagine his delicacy, and the passion he was in at their laughing!

WALPOLE

The fixed bath, except at spas, was almost unknown – Dr Johnson observed of baths, 'I hate immersion' – and Byron was still quite proud of building a bathroom at Newstead in the nineteenth century. Until the days of Jenner, most people were disfigured by smallpox, and the lack of reliable artificial teeth, though this convenience did exist, produced the Punch-and-Judy profile in old age.

In difficult circumstances, however, the aristocracy did its best. Tooth powder was used, and the choice of scents included Spirit of Ambergris, Otto of Roses, Aqua Mellis, and Cordova Water. If a footman touched the sugar for the lemonade with his fingers, even the slovenly Dr Johnson would throw the glass out of the window. They shifted their clothes frequently, and these were well washed at home. Johnson decided that when he kept a seraglio 'the ladies should all wear linen gowns – or cotton ... I would have no silk; you cannot tell when it is clean. . . . Linen detects its own dirtiness.' In later days Brummell insisted on 'country washing'. Their soaps were Joppa, Genoa, Irish, Bristol, Windsor, Black, and Liquid. They kept up a diligent campaign against fleas, pared their finger-nails with penknives, used scent with powder, and paid attention to their hair. The heads were shaved for the wig or the natural hair worn in a queue, the powder being sometimes tinted when *en grande toilette*.

The Prince de Kaunitz, who wore satin stays, passed a portion of every morning in walking up and down a room in which four valets puffed a cloud of scented powder, but each of a different colour, in order that it might fall and amalgamate into the exact *nuance* that best suited their master's taste.

CAPTAIN JESSE

The British Army, in the third George's reign, used 6,500 tons of flour for powdering every year.

England was then in advance of the Continent. The jeer at the eighteenth century, that its grandeur was in close proximity to a cess-pit, was only true of the court of Versailles. On the Continent the diamond necklace and the *vaso di notte* might be side by side, but English tourists complained of this, or reported it as abnormal.

She [a French domestic] had the modesty to address herself to me, as understanding her Language, to desire me to beg one of the Sailors to give her a Chamber Pot: upon which, thinking she was sick, as many were upon the Deck, I advised her to go to the Side of the Ship, and my Servant should hold her gown for Fear of tumbling over Board: but she directly told me, that however practicable such a Situation might be for us, it would not suit her at all: and without more ado, or further Ceremony, *sans Façon, à la Françoise,* she plainly told me she wanted a Chamber Pot, *pour faire lacher l'Eau*; these were her words: so I forthwith got her accomodated with one, which she, with as little Shame as Decency and Ceremony made immediate use of, before all the Company, and then gave it with the utmost *Sangfroid* and Indifference, to my Servant to empty it over Board for her. ... The Woman, when she saw me, and some others of the Company laughing at her Action, talked reasonably and sensibly upon the Occasion, as any one could: asked in plain, *gras* and indelicate Words, what any of us would do, if a sudden Griping should take us, and we should want to go to the Necessary House. But tho' the Woman's Arguments were right in the main, yet she mistook only in this single very material Point: that altho' what she had done was absolutely necessary, yet she might have made an excuse to have gone under Deck; and have done privately, and by herself, what she chose to do before all the World. But such is the Difference between English and French Education and Customs!

REV. WILLIAM COLE

Wraxall was astonished to find that the King of Naples would 'select his favoured individuals' to attend him on the *chaise percée*, observing: '*Sono ben pransato. Adesso bisogna un buona panchiata.*' The tedious and unpleasant Chevalier de Grammont – like Madame de Sévigné, one of Walpole's unaccountable enthusiasms from the previous century – had condescended to regard the court of Charles II as 'neither savage nor barbarous' (*ni grossière ni sauvage*). But now the boot was on the other foot. Horace Walpole, who would sit in the middle of the room at French inns, so far as possible from the wainscot, behind which he pretended that he could hear the 'old fleas talking of the days of Louis XIV', was disgusted with Versailles. 'The very footmen ... wait behind their master ... with a red handkerchief about their necks. Versailles, like everything else, is a mixture of parade and poverty.' 'There is one [barbarism], alas! I shall never get over – the dirt of this country: It is melancholy after the purity of Strawberry!'

I was giving him [Horace Walpole] a Description of my Entertainment at Madame Eynhouts, and particularly of her continual hawking and spitting about at Dinner time: he assured me it was the same in better Company, and told me that not two Days before, dining at one of the greatest tables in Paris, with a Great Deal of French Nobility, it was the same during the whole Course of their Dinner, and that in particular, a blind Lady of Fashion and great Distinction for her Wit and Understanding (Mme du Deffand), in the Middle of Dinner, while they were talking of the Dauphin's little Prospect of Recovery, assured the Company, that His Royal Highness had a greater Chance than they were aware of: that she had received a Letter that very Morning from Fontainebleau, giving her an Account that he had happily had a very stinking and foetid stool the evening before, and that in great Abundance. ... I should not have dwelt so long upon so filthy a Subject, but to shew the French in their true Light. ...

REV. WILLIAM COLE

Dr Johnson was even more emphatic than this. 'The French are a gross, ill-bred, untaught people; a lady there will spit on the floor, and rub it with her foot. What I gained by being in France was, learning to be better satisfied with my own country.'

Insanitary conditions on the Continent were still rampant during the Napoleonic wars, and they seem to have preyed upon the minds of the English nobility even more. Sir Thomas Styles, who had fought with fists against Shelley at Eton, got a commission in the 1st Foot Guards; but he complained after leaving Lisbon that the 'fleas and vermin on the march had nearly driven him mad'. Finally they did do so. 'Our doctor, Mr Bacot, a very kind fellow, anticipating brain fever, placed Styles in his camp bed, covered his head with wet towels, and desired his batman to watch over his master, and not to leave him for an instant. However, the servant fell asleep, and during the night poor Styles got out of bed, unlocked his trunk where his razors were kept, and with one of them deliberately cut his throat from ear to ear.' (Gronow.)

If England was cleaner than France, she was more comfortable – less stiff, that is to say – than middle Europe. There was a social ease which was frequently regretted by foreign ambassadors such as Sir Robert Murray Keith, in Vienna, where the hunting forests of Prince Lichtenstein had clean gravel walks and more than three hundred gamekeepers.

I have for this fortnight past [he wrote during a hot summer in 1776] been running about the country houses in the neighbourhood of this capital, without the most distant chance of enjoying one hour of that convivial gaiety which reigns at Mistley, Fawley, Wimbledon, Coombank, &c. Yet our noble personages are as civil and attentive as possible at their country seats; but still it is *otium cum dignitate* with a vengeance! and that same *dignitas* is to me a terrible damper of all social enjoyments. I have had my Andrew (a boy on the Grand Tour) for five days along with me at a princely castle, where he was powdered and perfumed at ten o'clock in the morning; then fetched a broiling walk in a *gilded* garden, dined in state, and after playing three grave rubbers at whist, we sallied forth for the evening's excursion in half a dozen coaches and six!

The most common foreign word used by the English letter-writers of the Age of Scandal was probably 'agrémen'. This was a measure of the English interests. They liked to have their *agrémens*, both physical and mental. They, if not their neighbours across the Channel, were interested in the comfortable pleasures of civilization, without its pomp. 'I did not mean to make my house so Gothick,' wrote Walpole, 'as to exclude conveniences and modern refinements in luxury.' And it was he, as an epicurean amateur of the humanities, who set the tone for the era.

The 'humanities': perhaps this was the key word for the seventeen-eighties. It was astonishing how much the upper classes knew. Fox was an authority on Cassandra of Lycophron, known to scholars as 'the Obscure': Walpole could read a blazon or print a fine edition or write about the history of Richard III: the classics had been flogged into everybody, so that the Latin poets were quoted as familiarly as educated people now quote Shakespeare: Greek was spouted in the House of Commons, though with no great success: it was in the royal library that Dr Johnson met the bibliophile King:

the main legacy of the coarse Sir Robert Walpole was a fabulous collection of pictures: all society went nightly to hear Handel or the Opera: the business of the country had actually been transacted between George I and his first Minister in dog latin: an Irish Earl had possessed the temerity to argue with Bentley: Selwyn, who was an ignoramus, wrote his unimpressive letters instinctively in a mixture of English, French, and Italian: in Paris, at Madame du Deffand's and at other salons, the visiting English talked almost as easily in the foreign tongue: and the scandalous Wilkes, who had belonged to a Hell-fire Club and who had set all Britain by the ears in Parliament, retired gracefully to edit Theophrastus.

Even in applied science, as opposed to the humanities, there was an attitude of learned dilettantism which is perhaps not unrefreshing when compared with the 'ologies' of our own day. Newton had shed his light upon physics: chemistry was concerned with phlogiston, and most of the other branches of learning were a matter for museums like junk-shops, for gentlemanly if dusty antiquaries, and for letters to the Royal Society. The typical biologist was not Linnaeus, not Ray, not Pennant, not even the aristocratic Buffon: it was George Edwards – who dedicated his first volume to the President and Fellows of the Royal College of Physicians, and a subsequent volume, as an afterthought, in enormous letters 'TO GOD' – followed, in tiny print, with the words 'from his resign'd, humble servant, Geo. Edwards'.

Everything in Edwards's 'natural history' was interesting rather than precise. From all directions the letters poured in to the learned publications – letters about wild boys found in Germany, about people whose skins had petrified like the Giant's Causeway, about ladies who gave birth to rabbits, about Siamese twins and thunderbolts and shifting bogs and Irish crowns and fat men and people with pigs' faces and why negroes were black. The full facts about bird migration were unknown even to the immortal Gilbert White – fortunately unknown, since it gave Dr Johnson the opportunity for one of his more prodigious belly-floppers. 'Swallows,' he explained tremendously, 'certainly sleep all the winter. A number of them conglobulate together, by flying round and round, and then all in a heap throw themselves under water, and lie in the bed of a river.'

But perhaps it was in medicine that their fancy and genteel experiment soared to the highest. Lady Frances Erskine, being struck with aphasia, tried learning a foreign language, thinking she might remember the new words, but the stratagem did not answer. Turnip water, with a poultice of mashed turnip, was used for chilblains. Another poultice used by Joseph Mydelton consisted of 'a top crust of a threepenny loaf toasted, then spread with soft soap put between a flannel made hot and applied to the part affected'. Lord Fermanagh, when ill for fifteen days in 1716, drank 'horse-dung posset daily'. The Chevalier Manfredi, 'an excellent doctor', recommended chickens fed on frogs to Lady Caroline Lamb. Bacon, the Royal Academician, 'eat freely of Ice Cream saying He knew of a Lady cured of a complaint in Her stomach by it'. 'I drank snail tea for breakfast,' wrote Torrington on 2 June 1792, 'for my chest is very sore.' When wetted by rain this nobleman used to rub himself with brandy or gin, which liquors he also used to sprinkle on his bed-clothes if he suspected them of being damp. At Biggleswade, in 1793, he also 'drank 3 pints [of port] every day, besides ½ pint of brandy' – and this without impairing his energies as a tourist in the least. 'This morning,' wrote John Baker in his diary on 2 October 1755, 'a negro child of Capn.

Dromgoole's found drowned in a tub of water, with its head down and heels up, how long they knew not; but brought to life by lighting a pipe of tobacco and sticking the small end in its fundament, and blowing it at the bowl.'

There was a good deal of insanity about, nobody knew why, and some of the cures for this malady were no less Draconic. 'Fuseli mentioned [to Farington] that a Medical man who attended Bedlam had said that the greatest number of those confined were *Women in love*, and the next class in respect of number was *Hackney* and *Stage Coachmen*, caused it was supposed by the constant shaking exercise to which they are subject which affects the *pineal gland*.' Musk was given to the mad King George as a medicine for insanity, but the poor fellow 'begged that it might be discontinued'. 'Dr Jenner,' wrote the artist Farington in 1796, 'has found that in *insane patients* He has moderated their violence by keeping them sick with tartar emetic. ... Camphor water is an excellent medicine for nervous complaints.' The waters of many spas, moreover, performed surprising cures. Those of Buxton particularly seem to have been successful. A Mrs Jessop, with a fortune of £16,000, 'was last year here', wrote Egmont in 1744, 'to be cured of a frenzy, wherein she succeeded. That good success brought her here again this year. She is now very orderly behaved and has got a lover.'

Among proprietary medicines, 'Velno's Vegetable Syrup' brought £5,000 a year to its proprietor, and was compounded of Goose-grass. The very greatest of all such brands was Dr James's Powder – 'a well-known specific unhesitatingly recommended by Horace Walpole, which seems to have polished off Oliver Goldsmith in 1774. Its active principle was antimony.' Next to this cure came laudanum and calomel. 'I'll tell your honour,' confided a country doctor to Sir Walter Scott, 'my twa simples are just laudamy and calamy!' 'But, John, do you never happen to kill any of your patients?' 'Kill? Ou ay, may be sae. Whiles they die and whiles no; – but it's the will o' Providence. Ony how, your honour, it wad be lang before it makes up for Flodden!'

Other medicines, according to C. E. Vulliamy, included Bacon's Cordial Essence of Russia Rhubarb, Dr Steer's famous Opodeldoc, Cordial Cephalic Snuff, Petastile Root, Balsam of Tolu, and 'an aphrodisiac known as the Balsamic Corroborant or Restorer of Nature which had received flattering encomiums from a certain Royal and several Noble Personages'.

Whatever else may be urged against them, the patients of the Age of Scandal were ready to try anything once.

Massage was called 'Champooing', and the Hon. E. Hamilton begged Lady Charleville not to be shy about going to a masseur called Mahomet. He was black, sixty years old, and, besides, her ladyship might wear a mask.

The new force, electricity, was attempted to be used medicinally, for instance by the diarist Barker; and John Yeoman, a country bumpkin, made trial of it in 1774:

then we was all Lactrified a Think is Imposable to describe. Its composed of a Mixture of cumbustables that if you Touch it the Fire flys out of it, besides You have Shuch Shudden Shock with it. We all hold hand in hand about 7 of us when I toucht it, and the Moment I was struck so hard in the Stomack that I could not stand, the Rest felt it as well as me, If there was 500 It would be all the same.

There was a belief that the breath of young women might be helpful in prolonging life. According to Mr Wadd, one physician actually took lodgings in a girls' boarding-school for this purpose. 'I am myself,' wrote

Philip Thicknesse in 1779, 'turned of sixty, and in general, though I have lived in various climates, and suffered severely both in body and mind, yet having always partaken of the breath of *young women, wherever they lay in my way*, I feel none of the infirmities, which so often strike the eyes and ears in this great city of sickness [Bath], by men many years younger than myself.'

Other cures were as peculiar, but less successful.

Lord Stafford had long had a weakness in his sight which seemed approaching fast to blindness, and among the other more common prescriptions was told by his physician that he must strictly abstain from all conjugal intercourse with his wife. This requirement he had adhered to for more than a twelvemonth when, notwithstanding, her Ladyship proved with child.

GLENBERVIE

The learned, elegant, but at the same time vigorous attitude to every facet of life had been shadowed forth by the gossips and cranks like Lord Hervey under the earlier Georges: it reached its height with Walpole: and persisted at least during the lifetime of Lord Byron – a lord, incidentally, who sorts rather oddly with the 'romantics' to whom he is usually assigned – whose *forte* was on the contrary in satire, whose letters were among the best of his works, who detested the shoddy raptures of Keats, who said of Horace Walpole, 'my aristocracy, which is very fierce, makes him a favourite of mine' – and the destruction of whose memoirs, by the pseudo-poet Moore, was one of the major tragedies of anecdotal literature.

*

Such was the cultural and scientific background to a period which has long proved fascinating to romantic novelists like Baroness Orczy, to film producers, and to producers of musical comedy. But it would be amusing to notice the reactions of a film producer, if he could really be moved into the Age of Scandal by a time machine.

For one thing, he would probably find some difficulty in understanding what was said to him. The difference in accent between a duke of the 1950s and a duke of the 1750s would be at least as great as the difference between a Cockney accent and a Devonshire one now. Rhymes which were perfect in those days have become what they call 'eye-rhymes' today, so that it is possible to reconstruct from them something of the way in which people once spoke. Everybody knows that 'tea' was pronounced 'tay'. 'Spoil' rhymed with 'mile'.

> Sally, Sally, don't deny,
> But for God's sake tell me why
> You have flirted so to spoil
> That once lovely youth, Carlisle?

It is curious [wrote Samuel Rogers] how fashion changes pronunciation. In my youth everybody said 'Lonnon', not 'London'. Fox said 'Lonnon' to the last; and so did Crowe. The now fashionable pronunciation of several words is to me at least very offensive: 'cóntemplate' is bad enough; but 'bálcony' makes me sick.

The Prince Regent [according to Gronow] still said 'Obleege' for 'oblige', though this pronunciation was becoming unfashionable. John Kemble, who was teaching him elocution, exclaimed with exasperation, 'Sir, may I beseech your Royal Highness to open your Royal jaws and say "oblige"?'

Surnames as well as place-names received a different inflection. Mrs Thrale would have called Lord Byron 'Biron' and Horace Walpole pronounced Stowe to rhyme with 'plough'.

A producer who ventured into the past, in fact, might have been invited to drink tay on the balcóny with Lord

Biron, where he would have been obleeged to con-témplate the unspiled agrémens of Lonnon.

One of the earliest existing phonograph records is of a speech by Gladstone, who stands half-way between ourselves and the eighteenth century. It sounds already like a music-hall imitation of a comic clergyman. In the Age of Scandal itself, it seems reasonably certain that people spoke even more slowly, even more oratori-cally, with even more pauses for mental punctuation between the concessive clauses. They certainly read more slowly.

Another surprise for the producer would have lain in the matter of attitude. For a gentleman in Walpole's period was judged not only by his accent but also by his deportment, as if he were a ballet. It was literally true that a gentleman had to move in a stylized way. George III complained that Lord Liverpool's 'motions were never very graceful'. The fat Bubb-Doddington, when created Lord Melcombe, was found 'before a looking glass in his new robes, practising attitudes and debating with himself upon the most graceful mode of carrying his coronet'. (Unfortunately, on being presented to Queen Charlotte, his breeches 'in the act of kneeling down, forgot their duty, and broke lose from their moorings in a very indecorous manner'.)

Books like *The Dancing Master* mentioned by M. Delahaute provided 'the Rules required for walking, saluting and making bows in all kinds of company', with a chapter entitled 'How to take off your Hat and replace it'. Frenilly 'took a month's course of instruc-tion from the celebrated Petit, at twelve francs a lesson', in order to learn how to introduce himself to a 'circle'. 'It was by no means an inferior science to know how to enter a drawing-room in which some thirty ladies and gentlemen were sitting in a circle round the fire, with both assurance and grace; to penetrate this circle and to make a slight inclination as you walked round it; to make your way to your hostess, and to retire with dignity and without ruffling your fine clothes, for you were dressed in lace, and your hair was dressed in thirty-six curls, all powdered; you were carrying your hat under your arm, your sword reached to your heels, and you were armed with a huge muff, the smallest being two and a half feet wide!' They moved, said Gronow, 'with a studied dignity of posture'. The Marquis of Abercorn, though this was more a matter of etiquette than of posture, was 'stated to have always gone out shooting in his Blue Ribbon, and to have required his housemaids to wear white kid gloves when they made his bed'.

Food and drink, from the enormous quantity in which they were consumed, would have been another of the surprises for a modern mind, and there would have been a hundred lesser reasons to raise the eyebrows. For instance, the people themselves were smaller than we are. 'The increase in the height of our countrymen,' wrote Miss Hawkins in 1822, 'attests the superior good sense with which children are now reared.' 'From a study of the dresses that do remain,' writes an authority on clothes, 'we may form the opinion that men and women were on the whole smaller than they are today, the women slighter in build and the men more stocky.' A Duchess of Rutland must surely have been very slight, when she could compress her waist into the size of an orange and a half.

For the rest, the eye would be taken by scattered curiosities. Peas were correctly eaten with a knife. Forks had only three prongs. There were no dessert spoons. The games of ombre, picquet, basset, whisk, brag, and lanterloo at which they gambled were played with cards whose Kings, Queens, and Knaves had feet.

Throughout England [wrote the son of the duc de Lian-court in 1784] it is the custom to breakfast together, the meal resembling a dinner or supper in France. The com-monest breakfast hour is 9 o'clock and by that time the ladies are fully dressed with their hair properly done for the day. Breakfast consists of tea and bread and butter in various forms. In the houses of the rich you have coffee, chocolate and so on. The morning newspapers are on the table and those who want to do so, read them during breakfast, so that the conversation is not of a lively nature. At 10 o'clock or 10.30 each member of the party goes off on his own pur-suit – hunting, fishing or walking. So the day passes till 4 o'clock but at 4 o'clock precisely you must present your-self in the drawing-room with a great deal more ceremony than we are accustomed to in France. This sudden change of social manners is quite astonishing and I was deeply struck by it. In the morning you come down in riding-boots and a shabby coat, you sit where you like, you behave exactly as if you were by yourself, no one takes any notice of you, and it is all extremely comfortable. But in the evening, unless you have just arrived, you must be well-washed and well-groomed. The standard of politeness is uncomfortably high – strangers go first into the dining-room and sit near the hostess and are served in seniority in accordance with a rigid etiquette. In fact for the first few days I was tempted to think that it was done for a joke.

Dinner is one of the most wearisome of English ex-periences, lasting, as it does, for four or five hours. The first two are spent in eating and you are compelled to exercise your stomach to the full in order to please your host. He asks you the whole time whether you like the food and presses you to eat more, with the result that, out of pure politeness, I do nothing but eat from the time that I sit down until the time when I get up from the table.

The courses are much the same as in France except that the use of sauce is unknown in the English kitchen and that one seldom sees a *ragout*. All the dishes consist of various meats either boiled or roasted and of joints weighing about twenty or thirty pounds.

After the sweets, you are given water in small bowls of very clean glass in order to rinse out your mouth – a custom which strikes me as extremely unfortunate. The more fashionable folk do not rinse out their mouths, but that seems to me even worse; for if you use the water to wash your hands, it becomes dirty and quite disgusting. This ceremony over, the cloth is removed and you behold the most beautiful table that it is possible to see. It is indeed remarkable that the English are so much given to the use of mahogany; not only are their tables generally made of it, but also their doors and seats and the handrails of their staircases. Yet it is just as dear in England as in France. It is a matter which I do not pretend to understand, but I am inclined to think that the English must be richer than we are; certainly I have myself observed not only that everything costs twice as much here as in France but that the English seize every opportunity to use things which are expensive in themselves. At all events, their tables are made of the most beautiful wood and always have a brilliant polish like that of the finest glass. After the removal of the cloth, the table is covered with all kinds of wine, for even gentlemen of modest means always keep a large stock of good wine. On the middle of the table there is a small quantity of fruit, a few biscuits (to stimulate thirst) and some butter, for many English people take it at dessert.

At this point all the servants disappear. The ladies drink a glass or two of wine and at the end of half an hour all go out together. It is then that real enjoyment begins – there is not an Englishman who is not supremely happy at this particular moment. One proceeds to drink – sometimes in an alarming measure. Everyone has to drink in his turn, for the bottles make a continuous circuit of the table and the host takes note that everyone is drinking in his turn. After this has gone on for some time and when thirst has become an inadequate reason for drinking, a fresh stimulus is supplied by the drinking of 'toasts', that is to say, the host begins by giving the name of a lady; he drinks to her health and everyone is obliged to do likewise. After the host someone else gives a toast and everyone drinks to the health of everyone else's lady. Then each member of the party names some man and the whole ceremony begins again. If more drinking is required, fresh toasts are always ready to hand; politics can supply plenty – one drinks to the health of Mr Pitt or Mr Fox or Lord North ... This is the time that I like best: Conversation is as free as it can be, everyone expresses his political opinions with as much frankness as he would employ upon personal subjects. Sometimes conversation becomes extremely free upon highly indecent topics – complete licence is allowed and I have come to the conclusion that the English do not associate the same ideas with certain words that we do. Very often I have heard things mentioned in good society which would be in the grossest taste in France. The sideboard too is furnished with a number of chamber pots and it is a common practice to relieve oneself whilst the rest are drinking; one has no kind of concealment and the practice strikes me as most indecent.

At the end of two or three hours a servant announces that tea is ready and conducts the gentlemen from their drinking to join the ladies in the drawing-room, where they are usually employed in making tea and coffee. After making tea, one generally plays whist, and at midnight there is cold meat for those who are hungry. While the game is going on, there is punch on a table for those who want it.

I have entered into these details of my experiences at Euston, where I stayed with the Duke of Grafton, because the manner of life is the same throughout England and the English manner being very different from our own, some details concerning it may be of interest.

In the short time that has elapsed between the eighteenth and twentieth centuries, a physiological change has taken place in the human body. It has not only grown bigger, but it also moves itself faster – not merely by mechanical means, but of itself. It changes its positions faster – no 'studied gestures' – runs faster – as one can see by looking at athletic records – boxes faster – for the endless rounds of an eighteenth-century match often had only one blow really delivered – speaks faster, reads faster, and even eats faster. The eighteenth century managed to eat so much more than we do because it ate more slowly. It could drink more, by drinking all night. Old Lady Dorothy Nevill, who was born in the reign of George IV, survived to complain in 1910 because 'everything is served at such lightning speed that it is as much as one can do to swallow the few mouthfuls called dinner before one's plate has been snatched away. The whole system of these hurried modern meals is uncomfortable and unhealthy.' It would be interesting to find out whether the pulse rate has gone up.

CHAPTER THREE

Royal Gossip

THE central feature was that the writers were patrician.
The aristocracy was a compact body, less numerous
than the peerage of the present day, and it was accustomed to foregather at fixed times and places. When
George III's reign began, there were only 174 peers
(there are nearly a thousand now). There were 'seasons'
at Bath or at Tunbridge Wells or in London, then small
enough for its society to be a single unit, and everybody
met at the Drawing-rooms and at the Birthdays of the
royal family. Their literature was one of personalities.
Great thoughts on large political or on moral issues
were absent, leaving only the trivialities of life and the
anecdotes about character which are nowadays the bane
of serious historians. The nature of the 'bootikins' worn
by Horace Walpole for his gout, or the problem of what
Dr Johnson used to do with his dried orange-peel, were
the core of the age. Horry's bootikins, it has been suspected, were bed-socks made of oiled silk outside and
wool within. The orange-peel question, though eluci-
dated in the 358th letter in Mrs Piozzi's collection, still
remains a vexing mystery to many people in 1950. It
came to a head in 1775.

Next morning [says Boswell] I won a small bet from Lady
Diana Beauclerk, by asking him as to one of his particulari-
ties, which her ladyship said I durst not do. It seems he had
been frequently observed at the Club to put into his pocket
the Seville oranges, after he had squeezed the juice of them
into the drink which he made for himself. Beauclerk and

Garrick talked of it to me, and seemed to think that he had a strange unwillingness to be discovered. We could not divine what he did with them; and this was the bold question to be put. I saw on his table the spoils of the preceding night, some fresh peels nicely scraped and cut into pieces. 'Oh, Sir,' said I, 'I now partly see what you do with the squeezed oranges which you put in your pocket at the Club.' JOHNSON: 'I have a great love for them.' BOSWELL: 'And pray, Sir, what do you do with them? You scrape them, it seems, very neatly, and what next?' JOHNSON: 'Let them dry, Sir.' BOSWELL: 'And what next?' JOHNSON: 'Nay, Sir, you shall know their fate no further.' BOSWELL: 'Then the world must be left in the dark. It must be said,' assuming a mock solemnity, 'he scraped them and let them dry; but what he did with them next he never could be prevailed upon to tell.' JOHNSON: 'Nay, Sir, you should say it more emphatically: – he could not be prevailed upon, even by his dearest friends, to tell.'

The prime subject for conversation, however, was the idiosyncrasy of the reigning monarch, rather than of his subjects. The literate aristocrats surrounded him on formal occasions several times a year. Twice a week some part of them lined the walls at the levee, while he walked round the room with the Queen, saying something appropriate to everybody who had come.

*

Horace Walpole met five kings, though he did not live to see the last two on the throne. His recollection of the first was clear but meagre, for he had been only ten years old at presentation.

Accordingly [he wrote as an old man, for the amusement of his beloved Misses Berry], the night but one before the King began his last journey, my mother carried me at ten at night to the apartment of the Countess of Walsingham on the ground floor, towards the garden of St James's, which opened into that of her aunt the Duchess of Kendal's. . . .

Notice being given that the King was come down to supper, Lady Walsingham took me alone into the Duchess's ante-room, where we found alone the King and her. I knelt down and kissed his hand. He said a few words to me, and my conductress led me back to my mother.

The person of the King is as perfect in my memory as if I saw him but yesterday. It was that of an elderly man, rather pale, and exactly like his pictures and coins; not tall; of an aspect rather good than august; with a dark tie-wig, a plain coat, waistcoat, and breeches of snuff-coloured cloth, with stockings of the same colour, and a blue riband over all. So entirely was he my object that I do not believe I once looked at the Duchess; but as I could not avoid seeing her on entering the room, I remember that just beyond his Majesty stood a very tall, lean, ill-favoured old lady; but I did not retain the least idea of her features, nor know what the colour of her dress was.

George the First [wrote the Earl of Chesterfield] was an honest, dull, German gentleman . . . lazy and inactive even in his pleasures, which were therefore lowly sensual. . . . He was diffident of his own parts, which made him speak little in public, and prefer in his social, which were his favourite, hours the company of wags and buffoons. Even his mistress, the dutchess of Kendal, with whom he p⸬sed most of his time, and who had all influence over him, was very little above an idiot . . . His views and affections were singly confined to the narrow compass of electorate; England was too big for him. If he had nothing great as a king, he had nothing bad as a man; and if he does not adorn, at least he will not stain the annals of this country. In private life he would have been loved and esteemed as a good citizen, a good friend, and a good neighbour.

Lady Mary Wortley Montagu added to this description, about his relations with the Schulemberg – his mistress who was created Duchess of Kendal – that 'he often went to her apartments to cut paper, which was his chief employment there', and Walpole capped the character-sketch by noting that he was superstitious. George I had been told that he would die within a year of his imprisoned wife, Sophia Dorothea, and she had died before the journey on which he gave his audience to little Horace Walpole.

Most Germans are superstitious [wrote the child sixty years later], even such as have few impressions of religion. George gave such credit to the denunciation, that on the eve of his last departure, he took leave of his son and the Princess of Wales with tears, telling them he should never see them more. It was certainly his own approaching fate that melted him, not the thought of quitting for ever two persons he hated ... I do not know whether it was about the same period, that in a tender mood he promised the Duchess of Kendal, that if she survived him, and it were possible for the departed to return to this world, he would make her a visit. The Duchess, on his death (1727), so much expected the accomplishment of that engagement, that a large raven, or some black fowl, flying into one of the windows of her villa at Isleworth, she was persuaded it was the soul of her departed monarch so accoutred, and received and treated it with all the respect and tenderness of duty, till the royal bird or she took their last flight.

The next king of Walpole's, George II, was ruled by his wife, Queen Caroline. He was a touchy, comic, obstinate, small man, with a mania for being thought to be brave and prepotent. He was charming, because he was straightforward. Whether he was in a temper or not, he spoke from his heart. He did not lie about his mistresses to his wife, whom he adored, and his tantrums or his sulks, the small deceptions about his courage or transparent boasts and pathetic tears when Caroline died, were true to himself. Lord Hervey gave a vivid description of him, in relating an evening *à trois*, when the

King had come back from Hanover in a state of exasperation, suffering from the royal piles and furious at having been forced to leave his latest mistress behind him in that country.

His Majesty stayed about five minutes in the gallery; snubbed the Queen, who was drinking chocolate, for being always stuffing; the Princess Emily for not hearing him; the Princess Caroline for being grown fat; the Duke of Cumberland for standing awkwardly; Lord Hervey for not knowing what relation the Prince of Sultzbach was to the Elector Palatine; and then carried the Queen to walk, and be resnubbed, in the garden. ...

One evening among the rest, as soon as Lord Hervey came into the room, the Queen, who was knotting whilst the King walked backwards and forwards, began jocosely to attack Lord Hervey upon an answer just published to a book of his friend Bishop Hoadley's on the Sacrament, in which the Bishop was very ill treated; but before she had uttered half of what she had a mind to say, the King interrupted her, and told her she always loved talking of such nonsense and things she knew nothing of; adding, that, if it were not for such foolish people loving to talk of those things when they were written, the fools who wrote upon them would never think of publishing their nonsense, and disturbing the Government with impertinent disputes that nobody of any sense ever troubled himself about. The Queen bowed, and said, 'Sir, I only did it to let Lord Hervey know that his friend's book had not met with that general approbation he had pretended.' 'A pretty fellow for a friend!' said the King, turning to Lord Hervey. 'Pray what is it that charms you in him? His pretty limping gait' (and then he acted the Bishop's lameness), 'or his nasty stinking breath? – phaugh! – or his silly laugh, when he grins in your face for nothing, and shews his nasty rotten teeth? Or is it his great honesty that charms your Lordship? – his asking a thing of me for one man and, when he came to have it in his own power to bestow, refusing the Queen to give it to the very man for whom he had asked it? Or do you admire his conscience that makes him now put out a book that, till he was Bishop of Winchester, for fear his conscience might hurt his preferment, he kept locked up in his chest? Is his conscience so much improved ...' [etc. etc.]. 'My Lord, I am very sorry you choose your friends so ill; but I cannot help saying, if the Bishop of Winchester is your friend, you have a great puppy and a very dull fellow and a great rascal for your friend. It is a very pretty thing for such scoundrels, when they are raised by favour so much above their desert, to be talking and writing their stuff, to give trouble to the Government that has shewn them that favour; and very modest in a canting hypocritical knave to be crying, " *The Kingdom of Christ is not of this world*," at the same time that he, as Christ's ambassador, receives 6000L. or 7000L. a-year. But he is just the same thing ...' [etc. etc.].

During the whole time the King was speaking, the Queen, by smiling and nodding in proper places, endeavoured all she could, but in vain, to make her court by seeming to approve everything he said; and well, indeed, might she approve it, for it was almost word for word what she had said to Lord Hervey on this subject in the summer when the book first came out, which Lord Hervey, to flatter her, whilst she flattered the King, gave her to understand he remembered, by telling her very emphatically, when she asked him *what he had to say to all this*, 'Your Majesty knows already all I have to say on this subject;' and then added (to sweeten the King), 'but how partial soever I may be to my friend, I assure your Majesty I am not so partial to myself as to imagine, let his cause be ever so good, that I should be able to plead it with success against the very able counsel that I have just now heard draw up the charge on the other side.'

He then, in order to turn the conversation, told the King that he had that day been with a Bishop of a very different stamp, who would never, he dared to answer for him, disturb his Majesty's Government with writing ... (The Bishop of Rochester.) 'My Lord of Rochester carried us to Westminster Abbey to shew us a pair of old brass gates to Henry VII's Chapel, which were formerly overrun with rust and turned quite black, but are now re-cleaned, as bright as when they were first made, and the finest things of the kind I ever saw in my life.' Whilst Lord Hervey was going on with a particular detail and encomium on these gates – the Queen asking many questions about them, and seeming extremely pleased with the description – the King stopped the conversation short by saying, 'My Lord, you are always putting some of these fine things in the Queen's head, and then I am to be plagued with a thousand plans and workmen.' Then turning to the Queen, he said, 'I suppose I shall see a pair of these gates to *Merlin's Cave*, to complete your nonsense there.' (This Merlin's Cave was a little building so christened, which the Queen had lately finished at Richmond.) The Queen smiled, and said Merlin's Cave was complete already; and Lord Hervey, to remove the King's fears of this expense, said that it was a sort of work that if his Majesty would give all the money in his exchequer he could not have now. 'A propos,' said the Queen, 'I hear the Craftsman has abused Merlin's Cave.' 'I am very glad of it,' interrupted the King: 'you deserve to be abused for such childish silly stuff, and it is the first time I ever knew the scoundrel in the right.'

This the Queen swallowed too, and began to talk on something else, till the conversation (I know not by what transition) fell on the ridiculous expense it was to people, by the money given to servants, to go and stay two or three days with their acquaintance in the country; upon which the Queen said she had found it a pretty large expense this summer to visit her friends even in town. 'That is your own fault,' said the King; 'for my father, when he went to people's houses in town, never was fool enough to be giving away his money.' The Queen pleaded for her excuse that she had only done what Lord Grantham had told her she was to do: to which his Majesty replied, that my Lord Grantham was a pretty director; that she was always asking some fool or other what she was to do; and that none but a fool would ask another fool's advice. The Queen then appealed to Lord Hervey whether it was not now as customary to give money in town as in the country. He knew it was not, but said it was. He added, too, that to be sure, were it not so for particulars, it would certainly be expected from her Majesty. To which the King said, 'Then she may stay at home, as I do. You do not see me running into every puppy's house, to see his new chairs and stools. Nor is it for *you*,' said he, addressing himself to the Queen, 'to be running your nose everywhere, and trotting about the town to every fellow that will give you some bread and butter, like an old girl that loves to go abroad, no matter where, or whether it be proper or no.' The Queen coloured, and knotted a good deal faster during this speech than she did before, whilst the tears came into her eyes, but she said not one word. Lord Hervey (who cared not whether he provoked the King's wrath himself or not, provided he could have the merit to the Queen of diverting his Majesty's ill-humour from her) said to the King, that, as the Queen loved pictures, there was no way of seeing a collection but by going to people's houses. 'And what matter whether she sees a collection or not?' replied the King. 'The matter is, Sir, that she satisfies her own curiosity, and obliges the people whose houses she honours with her presence.' 'Supposing,' said the King, 'she had a curiosity to see a tavern, would it be fit for her to satisfy it? and yet the innkeeper would be very glad to see her.' 'If the innkeepers,' replied Lord Hervey, 'were used to be well received by her Majesty in her palace, I should think the Queen's seeing them at their own houses would give no additional scandal.' The King, instead of answering Lord Hervey, then turned to the Queen, and, with a good deal of vehemence, poured out an unintelligible torrent of German, to which the Queen made not one word of reply, but knotted on till she tangled her thread, then snuffed the candles that stood on the table before her, and snuffed one of them out; upon which the King, in English, began a new dissertation upon her Majesty, and took her awkwardness for his text.

These lectures meant nothing at all – as the Queen knew. When she was on her death-bed, and urged him to marry again, poor George was hardly able to sob out: '*Non, non, j'aurai des maîtresses.*' When she was dead, he passed every day, and all day ... in the apartments of the Princesses, and was only called from thence for a few minutes when any of the Ministers wanted to speak with him about business, whilst every new body who was admitted to him on these occasions threw him into a new flood of tears. ...

He was thoroughly unaffected in his conduct on this occasion ... for his sudden transitions from tears to smiles, from a sighing pensive silence to a loud talkative conversation on things foreign to what one imagined at other times engrossed his thoughts – the tender manner in which he related a thousand old stories relating to his first seeing the Queen, his marriage with her, the way in which they lived at Hanover, his behaviour to her when she had the small-pox, and his risking his life by getting it of her (which he did) rather than leave her; and the next moment talking, with the most seeming indifference and calmness, of her being opened and embalmed, of the method of her ladies and maids of honour keeping watch by the body, and all the minutiae relating to the regulation of the funeral; – I say his talking with so much emotion and concern of old stories, and with so little on present circumstances which affected everybody in the room but himself, and perhaps the more for their seeming to affect him so little, puzzled one's judgement of the situation of his mind extremely, and made it vary as often as these circumstances on which it was to be formed.

One day he came into the room at once weeping and laughing, and said, '*Vous me croirez fou, je crois, mais je viens de voir le pauvre Horace Walpole, et il pleure de si mauvaise grâce, qu'au milieu de mes larmes il m'a fait rire.*'

It was the other Horace Walpole, the letter-writer's uncle, who had pretended to cry so unconvincingly.

The King owned a handsome leg adorned with the Garter; when irritated he had been known to 'kick his hat and wig about the room'; he was particularly mean with his money, which was why he had been so cross with the Queen about her tips and about the expense of Merlin's Cave, and he personally presented Sir Robert Walpole with little more than a bad diamond with a flaw in it. He was thought to reward his mistresses by giving them sweepstake tickets.

Of George III, insatiably inquisitive, talkative, silly, repetitive, obstinate, hard-working, kind, and nobly, tragic, the best descriptions were in Boswell's account of his conversation with Dr Johnson, or in Fanny Burney's story of her meeting with him at Kew, when mad.

I had proceeded in my quick way, nearly half the round, when I suddenly perceived, through some trees, two or three figures. Relying on the instructions of Dr John [Willis], I concluded them to be workmen and gardeners; yet I tried to look sharp, and in so doing, as they were less shaded, I thought I saw the person of his Majesty!

Alarmed past all possible expression, I waited not to know more, but turning back, ran off with all my might. But what was my terror to hear myself pursued! – to hear the voice of the King himself loudly and hoarsely calling after me: 'Miss Burney! Miss Burney!'

I protest I was ready to die. I knew not in what state he might be at the time; I only knew the orders to keep out of his way were universal; that the Queen would highly disapprove of any unauthorized meeting, and that the very action of my running away might deeply, in his present irritable state, offend him. Nevertheless, on I ran, too terrified to stop, and in search of some short passage, for the garden is full of little labyrinths, by which I might escape.

The steps still pursued me, and still the poor hoarse and altered voice rang in my ears – more and more footsteps resounded frightfully behind me – the attendants all running, to catch their eager master, and the voices of the two Doctor Willises loudly exhorting him not to heat himself so unmercifully.

Heavens, how I ran! ...

Soon after, I heard other voices, shriller, though less nervous, call out: 'Stop! Stop! Stop!'

I could by no means consent. ...

I knew not to what I might be exposed, should the malady be then high, and take the turn of resentment. Still, therefore, on I flew; and such was my speed, so almost incredible to relate or recollect, that I fairly believe no one of the whole party could have overtaken me, if these words, from one of the attendants, had not reached me: 'Doctor Willis begs you to stop!' 'I cannot! I cannot!' I answered, still flying on, when he called out: 'You must, ma'am; it hurts the King to run.' Then, indeed, I stopped – in a state of fear amounting to agony. I turned round, I saw the two Doctors had got the King between them, and three attendants of Dr Willis's were hovering about. ...

When they were within a few yards of me, the King called out: 'Why did you run away?'

Shocked at a question impossible to answer, yet a little assured by the mild tone of his voice, I instantly forced myself forward, to meet him. ...

The effort answered: I looked up, and met all his wonted benignity of countenance, though something still of wildness in his eyes. Think, however, of my surprise, to feel him put both his hands round my two shoulders, and then kiss my cheek!

I wonder I did not really sink, so exquisite was my affright when I saw him spread out his arms! Involuntarily, I concluded he meant to crush me: but the Willises, who have never seen him till this fatal illness, not knowing how very extraordinary an action this was with him, simply smiled and looked pleased, supposing, perhaps, it was his customary salutation!

He now spoke in such terms of his pleasure in seeing me,

that I soon lost the whole of my terror; astonishment to find him so nearly well, and gratification to see him so pleased, removed every uneasy feeling. ... What a conversation followed! When he saw me fearless, he grew more and more alive, and made me walk close by his side, away from the attendants, and even the Willises themselves, who, to indulge him, retreated. I own myself not completely composed, but alarm I could entertain no more.

Everything that came uppermost in his mind he mentioned; he seemed to have just such remains of his flightiness as heated his imagination without deranging his reason, and robbed him of all control over his speech, though nearly in his perfect state of mind as to his opinions.

What did he not say! He opened his whole heart to me – expounded all his sentiments, and acquainted me with all his intentions.

He assured me he was quite well – as well as he had ever been in his life; and then inquired how I did, and how I went on? and whether I was more comfortable? If these questions, in their implication, surprised me, imagine how that surprise must increase when he proceeded to explain them! He asked after the coadjutrix [Miss Burney was not on the best terms with her superior in the Queen's service, a German dragon called Mrs Schwellenberg], laughing, and saying, 'Never mind her – don't be oppressed – I am your friend! don't let her cast you down! I know you have a hard time of it – but don't mind her!'

Almost thunderstruck with astonishment, I merely curtsied to his kind 'I am your friend', and said nothing.

Then presently he added: 'Stick to your father – stick to your own family – let them be your objects.'

How readily I assented!

Again he repeated all I have just written, nearly in the same words, but ended it more seriously: he suddenly stopped, and held me to stop too, and putting his hand on his breast, in the most solemn manner, he gravely and slowly said: 'I will protect you! – I promise you that – and therefore depend upon me!'

I thanked him; and the Willises, thinking him rather too elevated, came to propose my walking on. 'No, no, no!' he cried, a hundred times in a breath; and their good humour prevailed, and they let him again walk on with his new companion.

He then gave me a history of his pages, animating almost into a rage, as he related his subjects of displeasure with them, particularly with Mr Ernst, who, he told me, had been brought up by himself. I hope his ideas upon these men are the result of the mistakes of his malady.

Then he asked me some questions that very greatly distressed me, relating to information given him in his illness, from various motives, but which he suspected to be false, and which I knew he had reason to suspect; yet was it most dangerous to set anything right, as I was not aware what might be the views of their having been stated wrong. I was as discreet as I knew how to be, and I hope I did no mischief; but this was the worst part of the dialogue.

He next talked to me a great deal of my dear father, and made a thousand inquiries concerning his *History of Music*. This brought him to his favourite theme, Handel; and he told me innumerable anecdotes of him, and particularly that celebrated tale of Handel's saying of himself, when a boy: 'While that boy lives, my music will never want a protector.' And this, he said, I might relate to my father.

Then he ran over most of his oratorios, attempting to sing the subjects of several airs and choruses, but so dreadfully hoarse that the sound was terrible.

Dr Willis, quite alarmed at this exertion, feared he would do himself harm, and again proposed a separation. 'No! No! No!' he exclaimed, 'not yet; I have something I must just mention first.'

Dr Willis, delighted to comply, even when uneasy at compliance, again gave way.

The good King then greatly affected me. He began upon my revered old friend, Mrs Delany; and he spoke of her with such warmth – such kindness! 'She was my friend!' he cried, 'and I loved her as a friend! I have made a

53

memorandum when I lost her – I will shew it to you.'

He pulled out a pocket-book, and rummaged some time, but to no purpose.

The tears stood in his eyes – he wiped them, and Dr Willis again became very anxious. 'Come, sir,' he cried, 'now do come in and let the lady go on her walk – come, now, you have talked a long while – so we'll go in – if your Majesty pleases.'

'No, no!' he cried, 'I want to ask her a few questions; I have lived so long out of the world, I know nothing!' He then told me he was very much dissatisfied with several of his state officers, and meant to form an entire new establishment. He took a paper out of his pocket-book, and shewed me his new list.

This was the wildest thing that passed; and Dr John Willis now seriously urged our separating; but he would not consent; he had only three more words to say, he declared, and again he conquered.

He now spoke of my father, with still more kindness, and told me he ought to have had the post of Master of the Band, and not that poor little musician Parsons, who was not fit for it: 'But Lord Salisbury,' he cried, 'used your father very ill in that business, and so he did me! However, I have dashed out his name, and I shall put your father's in – as soon as I get loose again!'

This again – how affecting was this!

'And what,' cried he, 'has your father got at last? Nothing, but that poor thing at Chelsea? Oh, fie! fie! fie! But never mind! I will take care of him! I will do it myself!'

Then presently he added: 'As to Lord Salisbury, he is out already, as this memorandum will shew you, and so are many more. I shall be much better served; and when once I get away, I shall rule with a rod of iron!' This was very unlike himself, and startled the two good doctors, who could not bear to cross him, and were exulting at my seeing his great amendment, but yet grew quite uneasy at his earnestness and volubility. Finding we now must part, he stopped to take leave, and renewed again his charges about the coadjutrix. 'Never mind her!' he cried, 'depend upon me! I will be your friend as long as I live! – I here pledge myself to be your friend!' And then he saluted me again just as at the meeting, and suffered me to go on.

The middle-aged, maidenly, and short-sighted Alice, with her White King rummaging for the memorandum that might as well have been a hay-sandwich: one wonders whether Charles Dodgson could have been a reader of Fanny Burney, and whether he suspected that her meeting with the King, for all its running, was not entirely disingenuous? What can have been at the back of her head? Did she want to be his Du Barry? They would have made an excellent pair.

George III 'got loose again', as he had hoped, but he was subject to returning and to more frequent attacks. Thirty years later, the poor, good old man of eighty-one, blind and deaf and witless – so that they had to lift his chair as the only signal to the imprisoned brain within – died officially, as he had long been dead in practice. It seems impossible to leave him without giving the last paragraph of Jesse's 'Life':

The coffin having been lowered into the grave, and the dust thrown upon it, Garter-King-at-Arms proclaimed the titles of the deceased. Once more the volumed tones of the organ pealed along the vaulted roof and through the fretted aisles. [It was his beloved Handel: 'I know that my Redeemer liveth.'] The mourners re-arranged themselves, and departed nearly in the order in which they came. The solemn ceremony was at an end. The soldiers, who had lined the aisles, extinguished their tapers and retired. Many persons, indeed, lingered to look down on the coffin and its splendid paraphernalia. Soon, however, the last faint note of the organ died away in the distance; the last straggler withdrew through the ancient Gothic portal; and then the once powerful and flattered monarch was left alone in a darkness and silence, not more awful, perhaps, but even more desolate, than had lately over-shadowed him in the neighbouring towers of the Plantagenets.

George IV, the 'first gentleman in Europe', who had signed himself 'Florizel' when wooing an actress in the part of Perdita – whom he subsequently abandoned – and who grew fat and alcoholic before he went to pieces altogether, was best described by Lord Malmesbury and in the Greville, Creevey, and other papers. Considered a poltroon by nearly everybody – and his constantly broken word, his trick of being bled by a physician in order to look pale and interesting when pressing an affair of the heart, and his self-inflicted flesh wound when pretending to commit suicide for the love of Mrs Fitzherbert, these certainly did not tend to raise his reputation – yet there was something to be said for the impulsive Regent after all. The mad King, his father, however kind to his subjects, had been a bad parent, as all the Hanovers were.

His mother [said Dr Doran of Florizel] had been his first governess; and at eight years of age he had been delivered by his father to Dr Markham and Cyril Jackson, with the injunction to treat him as they would any private gentleman's son, and to flog him whenever he deserved it. The prince ... took the earliest opportunity of shewing his antagonism against his father ... The young prince's preceptors were changed in 1776. Lord Bruce became governor in place of Lord Holdernesse; but he retired almost immediately, vexed, it is said, at the prince having detected him in the commission of a false quantity. Bishop Hurd and the Rev. Mr Arnold ... adopted the old plan of severity; but on endeavouring to carry it into effect, when the high-spirited boys were considerably advanced in their teens, one or both of the royal pupils turned on their preceptor, Arnold, who was about to most grossly castigate them, tore the weapon from his hand, and roughly administered to him the punishment with which they themselves had been threatened.

Another of the third George's sons, the Duke of Sussex, had been flogged for having asthma, and the Princess Sophia told the Hon. Amelia Murray 'that she had seen her two eldest brothers, when they were boys of thirteen and fourteen, held by their arms to be flogged like dogs, with a long whip!' George III, who thought it his duty to be present at these castigations, was only trying to be democratic, and to give his children the same sort of education as was enjoyed by his other subjects; but it was a mistaken liberalism in the case of Florizel.

Unwisely brought up, badly in debt, entangled with a morganatic marriage, and surrounded by cads, the unfortunate Prince of Wales (George IV) was married to Caroline of Brunswick, whom he had never seen.

I [said Lord Malmesbury, whose surname had been Harris before he was raised to the peerage], according to the established etiquette, introduced (no one else being in the room) the Princess Caroline to him. She very properly, in consequence of my saying to her it was the right mode of proceeding, attempted to kneel to him. He raised her (gracefully enough) and embraced her, said barely one word, turned round, retired to a distant part of the apartment, and calling me to him, said: 'Harris, I am not well; pray, get me a glass of brandy.'

Malmesbury recommended a glass of water, for the future King was a little drunk already – but it is fair to point out that his intended bride suffered from what is now called body odour. He retired without another word – leaving Caroline to exclaim, '*Mon Dieu, est-ce que le prince est toujours comme cela?*' – and he was quite drunk at the marriage.

'Damn the west! and damn the east! and damn

Wellington,' he cried in later life, in agony, during a discussion of the Duke's victories at various points of the compass. 'The question is, *how am I to get rid of this damned Princess of Wales?*'

I had heard a great deal [wrote Creave] of the Prince's drinking, but, during the time that I speak of, I never saw him the least drunk but once, and I was myself pretty much the occasion of it. We were dining at the Pavilion, and poor Fonblanque, a dolorous fop of a lawyer, and a member of Parliament too, was one of the guests. After drinking some wine, I could not resist having some jokes at Fonblanque's expense, which the Prince encouraged greatly ... the Prince said he should die if I did not stop ... In the evening, at about ten or eleven o'clock, he said he would go to the ball at the Castle, and said I should go with him. So I went in his coach, and he entered the room with his arm through mine, everybody standing and getting upon benches to see him. He was certainly tipsy, and so, of course, was I, but not much ... He used to drink a great quantity of wine at dinner, and was very fond of making any newcomer drunk by drinking wine with him very frequently, always recommending his strongest wines, and at last some remarkably strong old brandy which he used to call Diabolino.

The high-jinks at Brighton, in the famous Pavilion which the Regent had called into being, often rose to comic levels.

To return [said the same scandalmonger] to Sheridan at Brighton in the year 1805. His point of difference with the Prince being at an end, Sheridan entered into whatever fun was going on at the Pavilion as if he had been a boy, tho' he was then 55 years of age. Upon one occasion he came into the drawing-room disguised as a police officer to take up the Dowager Lady Sefton for playing at some unlawful game; and at another time, when we had a phantasmagoria in the Pavilion, and all were shut up in perfect darkness, he continued to seat himself upon the lap of

Madame Gerobtzoff (?) a haughty Russian dame, who made row enough for the whole town to hear her.

Mrs Creevey, who had a still finer eye for the ridiculous than had her husband, wrote to say that

When the Prince appeared [after dinner], I instantly saw he had got more wine than usual, and it was still more evident that the German Baron was extremely drunk ... Afterwards the Prince led all the party to the table where the maps lie, to see him shoot with an air-gun at a target placed at the end of the room. He did it very skilfully, and wanted all the ladies to attempt it. The girls and I excused ourselves on account of our short sight; but Lady Downshire hit a fiddler in the dining-room, Miss Johnstone a door and Bloomfield the ceiling. ... I soon had enough of this, and retired to the fire with Mac. ... At last a waltz was played by the band, and the Prince offered to waltz with Miss Johnstone, but very quietly, and once round the table made him giddy, so of course it was proper for his partner to be giddy too; but he cruelly only thought of supporting himself, so she reclined on the Baron.

The fact was that Florizel was a weak charmer with a tender heart, who could not help promising assistance to anybody that seemed to need it; and who consequently had to break his promises. His soft nature, when he was King, made it difficult to secure the signature to warrants of execution. 'There was a Council last Thursday,' wrote Greville, 'and the heaviest Recorder's report that was ever known, I believe; seven people left for execution. The King cannot bear this; and is always leaning to the side of mercy. Lord Tenterden, however, is for severity, and the Recorder still more so. It not unfrequently happens that a culprit escapes owing to the scruples of the King.' The Regent had started on the journey of life with the pathetic ambition to be loved for himself alone, only to find that princes could never be loved like that, because the subject's eye perceived preferment through the prince. It is in this light that we ought to read the descriptions of 'Punch' Greville. Their drunken and dishonoured figure was a disappointed man, romantic and disillusioned, an old Narcissus trying to forget the reflection of Silenus in the pool.

The King's indolence is so great that it is next to impossible to get him to do even the most ordinary business, and Knighton is still the only man who can get him to sign papers, &c. His greatest delight is to make those who have business to transact with him, or to lay papers before him, wait in his anteroom while he is lounging with Mount Charles or anybody, talking of horses or any trivial matter; and when he is told, 'Sir, there is Watson waiting,' &c., he replies, 'Damn Watson; let him wait.' He does it on purpose, and likes it. This account corresponds with all I have before heard, and confirms the opinion I have long had that a more contemptible, cowardly, selfish, unfeeling dog does not exist than this King, on whom such flattery is constantly lavished. He has a sort of capricious good-nature. . . .

The unfeeling dog had felt too much, and was tired of feeling.

The King complains that he is tired to death of all the people about him. He is less violent about the Catholic question, tired of that too, and does not wish to hear any more about it. He leads a most extraordinary life – never gets up till six in the afternoon. They come to him and open the window-curtains at six or seven o'clock in the morning; he breakfasts in bed, does whatever business he can be brought to transact in bed too, he reads every newspaper quite through, dozes three or four hours, gets up in time for dinner, and goes to bed between ten and eleven. He sleeps very ill, and rings his bell forty times in the night; if he wants to know the hour, though a watch hangs close to him, he will have his *valet de chambre* down rather than turn his head to look at it. The same thing if he wants a glass of water; he won't stretch out his hand to get it.

By the end of his life, what with hot rooms and cherry brandy, he was too fat and too ashamed of his stomach to go out, was partly blind and was afflicted with delusions. They were the delusions of what he would have liked to have been and done. Greville was not acute enough to see that they were pathetic. The King had convinced himself that he had commanded a division at Waterloo and that he had ridden a winning rac at Goodwood, to prove his 'bottom'.

One day when George the Fourth was talking about his youthful exploits, he mentioned, with particular satisfaction, that he had made a body of Troops charge down the Devil's Dyke (near Brighton). Upon which the Duke of Wellington merely observed to him, 'Very steep, sir.'

SAMUEL ROGERS

Most pathetic of all – and a proof of the profound love for his father which had wrecked his life by some unconscious tangle – he had convinced himself that he and George III had been models for child and parent. In point of fact, the insane King had once flown at his throat, and they had hated each other.

One day he was talking of the late King, and asserted that George III had said to himself, 'Of all the men I have ever known you are the one on whom I have the greatest dependence, and you are the most perfect gentleman.' Another day he said, 'that he recollected the old Lord Chesterfield, who once said to him, "Sir, you are the fourth Prince of Wales I have known, and I must give your Royal Highness one piece of advice: stick to your father; as long as you adhere to your father you will be a great and happy man, but if you separate yourself from him you will be nothing and an unhappy one"; and, by God (added the King), I never forgot that advice, and acted upon it all my life.' 'We all,' said the Duke, 'looked at one another with astonishment.'

When he was finally dead, with the dreadful cry of 'This is death! Oh God, they have deceived me!' there were found in his wardrobe all the coats, boots, and pantaloons of fifty years. He had remembered them all, and could call for any one of them at any moment. There were five hundred pocket-books, containing forgotten sums of money amounting to £10,000, together with countless bundles of women's love-letters and locks of hair. Greville was indignant about this, as he had been indignant when the King spent all his time altering the uniforms of the Guards and seeing more of his tailor, for that purpose, than he had seen of his Prime Minister. But the prerogative of the crown had already been hamstrung by the growth of parliamentary power, and there was little left for kings to do, unbidden, except to alter uniforms and count their clothes.

William IV lay almost outside the scope of the Age of Scandal, but there were good descriptions of him in Fanny Burney and in Greville. He was an honest tar with a foible for after-dinner speeches. He was at a Birthday, when young, in 1791:

After dinner Mrs Schwellenberg presided, attired magnificently. Miss Goldsworthy, Mrs Stainforth, Messrs de Luc and Stanhope dined with us; and, while we were still eating fruit, the Duke of Clarence [William IV] entered.

He had just risen from the King's table [George III's], and was waiting for his equipage to go home and prepare for the ball. To give you an idea of his Royal Highness's language, I ought to set apart a general objection to writing ... certain forcible words, and beg leave to shew you, in genuine colours, a Royal sailor.

We all rose, of course, upon his entrance, and the two gentlemen placed themselves behind their chairs, while the footmen left the room; but he ordered us all to sit down, and called the men back to hand about some wine. He was in exceeding high spirits and in the utmost good humour. He placed himself at the head of the table, next to Mrs Schwellenberg, and looked remarkably well, gay, and full of sport and mischief, yet clever withall as well as comical.

'Well, this is the first day I have ever dined with the King at St James's on his birthday. Pray, have you all drunk his Majesty's health?'

'No, your Roy'l Highness: your Roy'l Highness might make dem do dat,' said Mrs Schwellenberg.

'Oh, by – will I! Here you (to the footman); bring champagne! I'll drink the King's health again, if I die for it! Yet, I have done pretty well already: so has the King. I promise you! I believe his Majesty was never taken such good care of before. We have kept his spirits up, I promise you; we have enabled him to go through his fatigues; and I should have done more still, but for the ball and Mary – I have promised to dance with Mary!'

Princess Mary made her first appearance at Court today. ...

Champagne being now brought for the Duke, he ordered it all round. When it came to me I whispered to Westerhaults to carry it on: the Duke slapped his hand violently on the table and called out: 'Oh, by –, you shall drink it.'

There was no resisting this. We all stood up, and the Duke sonorously gave the Royal toast.

'And now,' cried he, making us all sit down again, 'where are all my rascals of servants? I shan't be in time for the ball; besides, I've got a deuced tailor waiting to fix on my epaulette! Here, you, go and see for my servants! d'ye hear? Scamper off!'

Off ran William.

'Come, let's have the King's health again. De Luc, drink it. Here, champagne to de Luc!'

I wish you could have seen Mr de Luc's mixed simper – half pleased, half alarmed. However, the wine came and he drank it, the Duke taking a bumper for himself at the same time.

'Poor Stanhope!' cried he: 'Stanhope shall have a glass too! Here, champagne! what are you all about? Why don't you give champagne to poor Stanhope?'

Mr Stanhope, with great pleasure, complied, and the Duke again accompanied him.

'Come hither, do you hear?' cried the Duke to the servants, and, on the approach, slow and submissive, of Mrs Stainforth's man, he hit him a violent slap on the back, calling out: 'Hang you! Why don't you see for my rascals?'

Away flew the man, and then he called out to Wester-haults: 'Hark 'ee! Bring another glass of champagne for Mr de Luc!'

Mr de Luc knows these Royal youths too well to venture at so vain an experiment as disputing with them; so he only shrugged his shoulders and drank the wine.

The Duke did the same.

'And now, poor Stanhope,' cried the Duke; 'give another glass to poor Stanhope, d'ye hear?'

'Is not your Highness afraid,' cried Stanhope, displaying the full circle of his borrowed teeth, 'I shall be apt to be rather up in the world, as the folks say, if I tope on at this rate?'

'Not at all! You can't get drunk in a better cause. I'd get drunk myself if it was not for the ball. Here, champagne! Another glass for the philosopher! I keep sober for Mary.'

'Oh, your Royal Highness!' cried Mr de Luc, gaining courage as he drank, 'you will make me quite droll of it if you make me go on – quite droll!'

'So much the better! so much the better! it will do you a monstrous deal of good. Here, another glass of champagne for the Queen's philosopher!'

Mr de Luc obeyed, and the Duke then addressed Mrs Schwellenberg's George. 'Here, you! you! why, where is my carriage? Run and see, do you hear?'

Off hurried George, grinning irrepressibly. . . .

Some talk then ensued upon the Duke's new carriage,

which they all agreed to be the most beautiful that day at Court. I had not seen it, which, to me, was some impediment against praising it.

He then said it was necessary to drink the Queen's health.

The gentlemen here made no demur, though Mr de Luc arched his eyebrows in expressive fear of consequences.

'A bumper,' cried the Duke, 'to the Queen's gentleman usher.'

They all stood up and drank the Queen's health.

'Here are three of us,' cried the Duke, 'all belonging to the Queen: the Queen's philosopher, the Queen's gentleman usher and the Queen's son; but, thank heaven, I'm nearest!'

'Sir,' cried Mr Stanhope, a little affronted, 'I am not now the Queen's gentleman usher; I am the Queen's equerry, sir.'

'A glass more of champagne here! What are you all so slow for? Where are all my rascals gone? They've put me in one passion already this morning. Come, a glass of champagne for the Queen's gentleman usher!' laughing heartily.

'No, sir,' repeated Mr Stanhope; 'I am equerry now, sir.'

'And another glass for the Queen's philosopher!'

Neither gentleman objected; but Mrs Schwellenberg, who had sat laughing and happy all this time, now grew alarmed, and said: 'Your Royal Highness, I am afraid for the ball!'

'Hold your potato-jaw, my dear,' cried the Duke, patting her; but, recollecting himself, he took her hand and pretty abruptly kissed it, and then, flinging it hastily away, laughed aloud, and called out: 'There! that will make amends for anything, so now I may say what I will. So here! a glass of champagne for the Queen's philosopher and the Queen's gentleman usher! Hang me if it will not do them a monstrous deal of good!'

Unfortunately, he failed to dance with Mary.

In 1811, in Greville, William IV was proposing toasts again as King, at a dinner which was remarkable for a tactful comment by the impenetrable Talleyrand.

The talk of the town has been about the King and a toast he gave at a great dinner at St James's the other day. He had ninety guests – all his Ministers, all the great people, and all the foreign Ambassadors. After dinner he made a long, rambling speech in French, and ended by giving as 'a sentiment', as he called it, 'The land we live in.' This was before the ladies left the room. After they were gone he made another speech in French, in the course of which he travelled over every variety of topic that suggested itself to his discursive mind, and ended with a very coarse toast and the words 'Honi soit qui mal y pense.' Sefton, who told it me, said he never felt so ashamed; Lord Grey was ready to sink into the earth; everybody laughed of course, and Sefton, who sat next to Talleyrand, said to him, '*Eh bien, que pensez-vous de cela?*' With his unmoved, immovable face he answered only, '*C'est bien remarquable.*'

*

Such were the monarchs who presided over the period of Horace Walpole. There was something warm and ridiculous about all of them, which would have been lost except for the gossip of the age. Whether it was George I appearing as a raven; or George II having a chair pulled from under him; or George III being greeted with the strains of *God Save the King* as he entered the sea from the royal bathing-machine at Weymouth; or George IV, when very fat, spraining his ankle while dancing the Highland Fling; or William dancing gaily with an admiral and delivering a course of lectures on adultery to the House of Lords – they had a genius for the unexpected. The fracas with George II's chair may be worth repeating. Walpole sent the news of it to Sir Horace Mann, in 1742.

There has been a great fracas at Kensington: one of the

Mesdames [the King's daughters] pulled the chair from under the Countess Deloraine [the King's favourite] at cards, who, being provoked that her Monarch was diverted with her disgrace, with the malice of a hobby-horse, gave him just such another fall. But alas! the Monarch, like Louis XIV, is mortal in the part that touched the ground, and was so hurt and so angry, that the Countess is disgraced, and her German rival remains in the sole and quiet possession of her royal master's favour.

At the same time, for all the absurdity, it was notable that Walpole's sovereigns were inclined to conform to the standard of culture enjoyed by their aristocracy. George I was said to have claimed that he was proud to rule in two countries which could boast of Leibnitz and Newton; George II wrote the finest love-letters Lord Hervey had ever seen; George III was a collector of books and a musician who considered that unmusical people were dumb; and George IV was a linguist, singer, art-patron, and dilettante, who, so Wraxall said, was 'competent to peruse the Greek, as well as the Roman poets and historians, in their own language'. William, however, 'Silly Billy', had been cheated of the family culture by his naval education. He, according to Beau Brummell, was 'only fit to walk about on a quarter-deck and cry "Luff!"'

CHAPTER FOUR

Bottom

IN the eighteenth century, but particularly under the Regency, a gentleman was expected to have 'bottom'. It was a word of composite meaning, which implied stability, and also what the twentieth century calls 'guts'. It meant being able to keep one's head in emergencies, and, in a financial sense, that one was backed by capital, instead of being an adventurer. Bottom, in fact, was synonymous with courage, coolness, and solidity. The metaphor was derived from ships.

Talking of a very respectable author, he told us a curious circumstance in his life, which was, that he had married a printer's devil. REYNOLDS: 'A printer's devil, Sir! Why, I thought a printer's devil was a creature with a black face and in rags.' JOHNSON: 'Yes, Sir. But I suppose he had her face washed, and put clean clothes on her. (Then looking very serious and very earnest.) And she did not disgrace him; – the woman had a bottom of good sense.' The word *bottom* thus introduced, was so ludicrous, when contrasted with his gravity, that most of us could not forbear tittering and laughing; though I recollect that the Bishop of Killaloe kept his countenance with perfect steadiness, while Miss Hannah More slily hid her face behind a lady's back who sat on the same settee with her. His pride could not bear that any expression of his should excite ridicule, when he did not intend it; he therefore resolved to assume and exercise despotick power, glanced sternly around, and called out, in a strong tone, 'Where's the merriment?' Then collecting himself, and looking aweful, to make us feel how he could impose restraint, and as it were searching his mind for a still more ludicrous word, he slowly pronounced, 'I say the *woman* was *fundamentally* sensible'; as if he had said, hear this now, and laugh if you dare. We all sat composed as at a funeral.

We are apt to forget how necessary the stoic and solid qualities must have been, in an age before anaesthetics and modern medicine. Childbirth had no palliatives then, and operations were performed either in full consciousness, or else with the patient inebriated, or else, it has been said, after stunning the sufferer with a mallet. 'Imagining that the dropsical collection of water which oppressed him might be drawn off by making incisions in his body', Dr Johnson took matters into his own hands and 'with his usual resolute defiance of pain, cut deep when he thought that his surgeon had done it too tenderly'.

Every day once at least [said Lord Hervey in describing Queen Caroline's fatal operation for a rupture] and some-times oftener, from the first of her being under the surgeons' hands, they were forced, or thought themselves so, to make some new incision; and before every operation of this kind which she underwent, she always used to ask the King if he approved what the surgeons proposed to do; and when he said they had told him it was necessary, and that he hoped she would consent to anything they thought so, she always submitted immediately, and suffered them to cut and probe as deep and as long as they thought fit, with the utmost patience, resignation and resolution. She asked Ranby once, whilst he was dressing her wound, if he would not be glad to be officiating in the same manner to his own old cross wife that he hated so much; and if any involuntary groans or complainings broke from her during the operations, she used immediately after to bid the surgeons not mind her, and would make them apologies for interrupting them with her silly complaints, when she knew they were doing all they could to help her. Poor Lord Digby [wrote Horace

Walpole in 1756] is likely to escape happily at last, after being cut for the stone, and bearing the preparation and execution with such heroism, that waking with the noise of the surgeons, he asked if that was to be the day? 'Yes.' – 'How soon will they be ready?' – 'Not for some time.' – 'Then let me sleep till they are.' He was cut by a new instrument of Hawkins, which reduces an age of torture to but one minute.'

In the preceding century Pepys had kept the day of his operation for the stone as an anniversary of the awful deliverance. At sea, a hundred years later, in the navy which Pepys had made, a part of the drill known as 'clearing decks for action' consisted in removing the seamen's chests to the middle of the aisle between the gun-ports. This was done by the Loblolly Men, who made a platform with the chests, on which the surgeons laid out their saws and chisels. When the action began, and the eighty-pound shot began to thump against the wooden walls, and to splinter them, and to enter, the Loblolly Men seized the casualties and hauled them screaming to the platform, where the surgeons sawed off any shattered limb as quickly as possible, tied up the arteries with silk – which was to be tugged daily, if the patient survived, until it rotted and came away – and dipped the stump in hot tar. Those who were too badly wounded were thrown overboard. Shelley's romancing friend Trelawny said that his ship, the *Superb*, was uniformly painted red inside at the period of Trafalgar, so that the blood would not show.

Not only were the physical facts of life formidable, but also the spiritual ones. Any husband had to be prepared to see his wife or children carried off, by smallpox before Dr Jenner and Lady Mary Wortley Montagu had made inoculation fashionable, or by childbirth, or by one of the peculiar diseases which then went by different names. The slaughter of bereavement, which kills the previous life of the survivor, was in wait for them. Five of Crabbe's seven children died; Gibbon was the sole survivor of seven siblings; four of Sterne's six brothers died; Gray was the only one who lived, from a family of twelve. Conditions had been even worse in earlier times. Defoe, writing in 1722, mentioned an Essex farmer then living with his five-and-twentieth wife, with a son of 35 who had already had fourteen.

The reason, as a merry fellow told me, who said he had had about a dozen and a half of wives (tho' I found afterwards he fibb'd a little) was this; that they being bred in the marshes themselves, and season'd to the place, did pretty well with it; but that they always went up into the hilly country, or to speak their own language into the uplands for a wife: that when they took the young lasses out of the wholesome and fresh air, they were healthy, fresh and clear, and well; but when they came out of their native air into the marshes among the fogs and damps, there they presently chang'd their complexion, got an ague or two, and seldom held it above half a year, or a year at most; and then, said he, we go to the uplands again, and fetch another.

To meet these adversaries, and also to meet the minor ones of gout and sudden death by highwaymen and the gallows which held out its arms for many crimes beside the one of murder – 200 offences were punishable by death in eighteenth-century criminal law – the faculty of Bottom was cultivated. It was felt that, if their heads were to be bloody, it would be a stay to find that they could keep them still unbowed. Those who could keep them so were admired; those who could not, were trained, so far as possible, to achieve the necessary resilience. Perhaps it was the first two Georges who had set the fashion. It was George II who had stood in front of his troops at Dettingen, after his horse had run away with him, with his sword advanced in the attitude of a fencing master, exclaiming in broken English: 'Now, boys, now for the honour of England; fire and behave bravely, and the French will soon run.' It was he who had persecuted Byng and Germaine for cowardice.

The earliest training for the faculty was appropriately concentrated on the physical bottom.

I was carried to Dublin [wrote Sir Jonah Barrington], and put to the famous schoolmaster of that day, Dr Ball, of St Michael-a-Powell's, Ship-Street; – and here my puzzling commenced in good earnest. I was required to learn the English Grammar in the Latin tongue; and to translate languages without understanding any of them. I was taught prosody without verse, and rhetoric without composition; and before I had ever heard any oration except a sermon, I was flogged for not minding my emphasis in recitation. To complete my satisfaction, – for fear I should be idle during the course of the week, castigation was regularly administered every Monday morning, to give me, by anticipation, a sample of what the repetition-day might produce.

It was related of Dr Parr that:

As the best boys were generally in requisition at lesson, of course they came under more frequent rebuke of the rod: but for the most part we all had our share; when a question was not answered in the first instance, it was put to every boy with 'you', 'you', 'you', &c., and the result too often was, '*I'll flog you all*': this was immediately done, and it was my business, as the last in the form, to assist in the operation; and then I came to the slaughter last, like Ulysses, but ere this the hand of the executioner was wearied, or his displeasure abated ... Some years ago, when I asked him whether he did not feel some compunction for having given us so much torture, he replied in a loud and good-natured tone, '*You rogue, it would be the worse for you, if I had you now.*'

Yet Samuel Parr considered himself, and was widely

considered, a liberal-minded person. He would never
flog a boy twice at the same lesson.

Dr Johnson declared that the awful Dr Busby
(1606–95), who had been the headmaster of Westminster School, used to say that his rod was his sieve,
and that whosoever could not pass through that was not
the boy for him. When he retired and was succeeded,
after Knipe or Matier, by Dr Freind, somebody wrote
the epigram:

> Ye sons of Westminster who still retain
> Your antient dread of Busby's awful reign,
> Forget at length your fears – your panic end –
> The monarch of the place is now a Freind.

Johnson himself was an ardent advocate of the birch,
and said that he owed his knowledge of Latin to the
plentiful flogging of his master, Mr Hunter. 'My master
whipt me very well. Without that, Sir, I should have
done nothing.' He told Mr Langton that while Hunter
was flogging his boys unmercifully, he used to say, 'And
this I do to save you from the gallows.' 'Children,' said
the Doctor, 'being not reasonable, can only be governed
by fear', and he proceeded to extenuate the activities
of a schoolmaster who was being prosecuted for cruelty
by explaining that 'no scholar has gone from him either
blind or lame'. In the previous century, Nathaniel
Eaton (d. 1674), the drunken master of Harvard College
in America, had awarded his pupils thirty stripes at a
time, and had beaten his usher for two hours with a
'walnut-tree plant big enough to have killed a horse'.
Dr Keate, the headmaster of Eton (1773–1852), flogged
more than eighty boys on one day, and only regretted
that he had not flogged more. A flogging was applied to
the buttocks with a birch, after the sufferer had placed
himself on a block, or been 'horsed' on another boy's

back, and, if this operation may have taken three minutes, Dr Keate must have been in action for four hours, 'He was,' said Kinglake, 'little more, if more at all, than five feet in height, and was not very great in girth, but in this space was concentrated the pluck of ten battalions. He had a really noble voice, and this he could moderate with great skill, but he had also the power of quacking like an angry duck.' Dryden had remembered the birch of one of these worthies 'to his dying day' – but had sent his two eldest sons to the same school – and it was said that another of them, who was accustomed to flagellate boys every morning according to a list provided, contrived to muddle his lists and whipped the confirmation class before the error was corrected. The poet Southey was expelled from West-minster in 1792, for writing against the beatings in the school magazine, and Lawrence, the great Governor-General of India, who went to school in 1811, said bitterly: 'I was flogged once every day of my life at school except one, and then I was flogged twice.'

It would be a mistake to waste too much sympathy on the average schoolboy, however. So effective was the encouragement of Bottom that full-sized rebellions broke out in more than one Public School, so serious that they had to be quelled by the military. The rebellion at Harrow, about Parr's claims to be headmaster, lasted for three weeks. The boys themselves entered into the spirit of the thing, and readers of *Tom Jones* or Lamb's essay on Christ's Hospital, or of *Tom Brown's Schooldays*, or of the various lives of the poet Shelley, will know enough about flogging and roasting and boxing-to-death-behind-the-chapel.

Samuel Rogers said that 'when Lord Holland was a schoolboy, he was forced, as a fag, to toast bread *with his fingers* for the breakfast of another boy. Lord H's mother sent him a toasting fork. His fagger broke it over his head, and still compelled him to prepare the toast in the old way. In consequence of this process his fingers suffered so much that they always retained a withered appearance.' Some of the fags survived, and, according to the inexorable law of nature, the survivors were the fittest.

Another way of learning to meet the undauntable ills of life was by pugilism. The snob Byron was proud to be seen in the company of a great boxer, Gentleman Jackson, his 'old friend and corporeal pastor and master' who had taught him the noble art. The respect paid to this fighter was sufficient to astonish Moore. Jackson's claims to fame were that he could lift $10\frac{1}{4}$ hundred-weight, could sign his name with an eighty-four pound weight tied to his little finger, and that he had been employed as a bodyguard at the coronation of Florizel, with eighteen other prizefighters dressed as pages. He had been the champion heavyweight of England for eight years, and had fought the famous battles with Mendoza, Fewterel, and George the Brewer. In short, he was worshipped for his Bottom; as well he might be. He had fallen during his fight with the Brewer in 1789, dislocating his ankle and breaking a bone in his leg, but had offered to finish the contest 'tied to a chair'. He lived to be seventy-seven.

The Fewterel engagement had been fought in the presence of the Prince of Wales – Florizel – and the world of fashion paid its homage to the quality of guts in the persons of these bruisers, in their stockings and knee-breeches of white, with torso bare like a side of beef and fist ungloved, who battered each other with solemn attention for twenty or thirty rounds, before they finally fell to the earth like the oak on Mount Avernus. In 1816, umpired by the Marquis of Queensberry,

Tom Oliver was carried from the ring after the thirty-second round 'in a state of stupor, and completely deprived of sight'. Painter *v.* Spring, in 1818, continued to the forty-second round. Bendigo and William Looney, 1837, remained upright for ninety-nine rounds.

Another facet of Bottom was the capacity to bet. 'Our ancestors were men of their hands,' said G. M. Trevelyan, 'who regarded a duel as the natural issue of a quarrel, and a bet as the most authoritative solution of an argument.' They did not find it convenient 'to spend twenty minutes in confuting a man who had so little faith in his own view that he would not back it with twenty guineas'. The wager was, according to this historian, a kind of *reductio ad absurdum*, or a cutting of the Gordian knot in controversy. When one man claimed that the world was round, and the other that it was flat, they might save themselves many hours of useless debate by backing their opinions financially, and by leaving it to the concrete decision. This was not, however, the spiritual basis of hazard and loo. In games of chance, at which, for instance, Charles James Fox lost one hundred and forty thousand pounds in three years, the young men of the period sought to harden their courage. It was Spartan to take one's fortune in one's hands and to risk it on the turn of pitch and toss. When they lost, they paid like men of honour, and it was then their business to start again at their beginnings, and never to breathe a word about their loss. It was in order to be a Man, in order to be a person of endurance, that they risked hereditary acres so desperately.

> Should the guardian friend or mother
>   Tell the woes of wilful waste;
> Scorn their counsel, scorn their pother,
>   You can hang or drown at last.

'The gaming,' wrote Walpole in 1770, 'is worthy the decline of an Empire. The young men lose five, ten, fifteen thousand pounds in an evening. Lord Stavordale, not one-and-twenty, lost eleven thousand last Tuesday, but recovered it by one great hand at hazard. He swore a great oath – "Now, if I had been playing deep, I might have won millions!"' When they had lost, to show that they were undaunted, they went peacefully to sleep with their heads on the table beside the dice-box like Selwyn, or pretended to do so. Fox nonchalantly sat down to read Herodotus. They had a special costume at Almack's. 'They began by pulling off their embroidered clothes, and put on frieze great-coats, or turned their coats inside outwards for luck. They put on pieces of leather such as are worn by footmen when they clean the knives, to save their laced ruffles; and, to guard their eyes from the light, and to prevent tumbling their hair, wore high-crowned hats with broad brims, and adorned with flowers and ribbons.' 'My Lord Rockingham and my nephew, Lord Orford, have made a match for five hundred pounds between five turkies and five geese to run from Norwich to London. Don't you believe in the transmigration of souls? And are you not convinced that the race is between Marquis Sardanapalus and Earl Heliogabalus?'

Betting, as opposed to the actual games of chance, became a mania. They betted on every subject, not only to back their opinions in the way mentioned by Trevelyan, but also out of bravado. They betted on the life-expectations of their own fathers. They betted that they could produce somebody fatter than the Duke of Cumberland, a bet which turned out to be difficult of solution owing to the delicacy of asking the Duke how much he weighed. They betted on the sex of the Chevalier d'Éon – in all some £110,000 – a series of bets which turned out to be impossible of solution, during his lifetime, owing to the reticence of the Chevalier. Thomas Whaley betted that he would jump from his drawing-room window into the first barouche that passed, and kiss the occupant. Another man betted that a human being could live under water, hired a desperado, sank him in some receptacle, and drowned him. He promptly hired another desperado to try again. When a passer-by fell down opposite Brooks's, apparently dead, they betted whether he was alive or not, and those who said that he was dead objected to the use of restoratives, as affecting the bet. One man betted that he would drive his tandem full speed so as to strike the wheels of the first seven oncoming vehicles on the Brentford Road – the 'bet' having by then become equivalent to the 'dare' – and he contrived to shave the wheels of all seven before he was overset, having proved his Bottom.

Fox-hunting was another sphere for courage. George III insisted that his children should be courageous on horseback, and believed that poor Florizel was a coward – which he was not, for he turned out to be dauntless about surgical operations.

Of Lord North [wrote Rose in his diary], his Majesty was beginning to speak in very favourable terms, when we were interrupted by the Princess Amelia, who with the other Princesses was riding behind us, getting a most unfortunate fall. The horse, on cantering down an inconsiderable hill, came on his head, and threw her Royal Highness flat on her face. She rose without any appearance of being at all hurt, but evidently a good deal shaken, and notwithstanding an earnest wish to avoid occasioning the slightest alarm, was herself not desirous of getting on horseback again. But the King insisted that she should, if at all hurt, get into one of the carriages, and return to Cuffnells to be bled, or otherwise mount another horse, and ride on. She chose the latter, and rode to Southampton, where she lost some blood unknown to the King. I hazarded an advice, that no one else would do, for her Royal Highness's return, which was certainly not well received, and provoked a quickness from his Majesty that I experienced in no other instance. He observed that he could not bear that any of his family should want courage; to which I replied I hoped his Majesty would excuse me if I said I thought a proper attention, to prevent the ill effects of an accident that *had* happened, were no symptom of a want of courage. He then said with some warmth – 'Perhaps it may be so; but I thank Heaven there is but one of my children who wants courage; and I will not name HIM, *because he is to succeed me.*'

Originally consisting in the patient pursuit of a fox, on steady horses assisted by contemplative and sagacious dogs, the hunt was accelerated in the eighteenth century until it had become a steeplechase. Squire Osbaldeston, in the next century, prostrate in a ditch with the bone of his leg sticking through the boot, after being jumped on by Sir James Musgrave, observed, 'I am so unlucky that I *think* I shall give up hunting' – and did not. Mytton's insane leaps were the cause of his popularity. Jorrocks was able to assert that the sport offered twenty-five per cent of the danger of war.

Drink was also taken as a form of endurance. Barrington gives an example of ten men who locked themselves in a room with a hogshead of claret and contrived to finish it, together with unspecified amounts of cherry brandy, in a week.

After drinking two-and-twenty bumpers [wrote Hickey], in glasses of considerable magnitude, the *considerate* President said, everyone might then fill according to his own discretion, and so *discreet* were all of the company that we continued to follow the Colonel's example of drinking nothing short of bumpers until two o'clock in the morning, at which hour each person staggered to his carriage or his palankeen, and was conveyed to town. The next day I was incapable of leaving my bed, from an excruciating headache, which I did not get rid of for eight-and-forty hours.

Two friends of Sir Philip Francis drank ten bottles of champagne and burgundy between them, at a sitting, without thinking it exceptional. 'I have drunk three bottles of port without being the worse for it,' said Dr Johnson. 'University College has witnessed this.' John Mytton took from four to six bottles a day, beginning while shaving. Tom Paine's weekly allowance of rum in 1808 was three quarts. Dr John Campbell informed Boswell, who disbelieved him, that he had once drank thirteen bottles of port at a sitting. Johnson, who rightly perceived that it depended on the length of the sitting, commented that it could be done 'if a man drinks very slowly and lets one glass evaporate before he takes another'. He summed up the whole question of Bottom in drinking with the magnificent apostrophe: 'No, Sir, claret is the liquor for boys; port for men; but he who aspires to be a hero (smiling) must drink brandy.'

Other forms of personal toughness were connected with the childish 'dare'. Mytton drove a chaise across country, by night, over hedge and ditch, till it collapsed: he jumped the iron railings of his park: he introduced a live bear at a dinner party: he galloped over a rabbit-warren to see whether his horse would fall, which it did: in the end, to cure the hiccoughs, he set light to his own nightshirt, and burned himself to death. It was to prove that he was not afraid.

Physical stamina was valued. Allardyce, born in 1779, once walked thirty miles grouse-shooting, dined at five, walked sixty miles to his house at Ury in eleven hours, attended to business, walked sixteen miles to Laurence Kirk, danced at a ball, returned to Ury by seven a.m., and spent the next day partridge-shooting, having travelled one hundred and thirty miles and been without sleep for two nights and three days.

The duel was the final test of Bottom. In Ireland it was a necessary diploma.

About the year 1777, the *Fire-eaters* were in great repute in Ireland. No young fellow could finish his education till he had exchanged shots with some of his acquaintances. The first two questions always asked as to a young man's respectability and qualifications, particularly when he proposed for a lady-wife, were, – 'What family is he of?' – 'Did he ever blaze?'

BARRINGTON

The strange thing about these people, in their aspect as they aspired to be heroes, was that their pistolling, boxing, flogging, gaming, boozing, daring, and enduring were combined with qualities which were so remote from being brutal. Their profuse tears in public, gentleness to blind old women like Madame du Deffand or Mrs Delaney, politeness in the act of fighting, tenderness for lap-dogs, and real enjoyment of literature, together with a hundred other forms of wit, culture, delicacy, and eccentricity, made it ridiculous to think of them as bruisers. Bottom was the quality still possessed by certain celluloid toys of our own century – but they are not modern, for Creevey's step-daughter had one which she called Fanny Royds, and Creevey said that it looked like Queen Caroline – which, being weighted with lead, spring upright when they have been pushed over. The *Oxford English Dictionary*, which defines the word in this sense as 'physical resources, "staying power", power of endurance; said esp. of pugilists, wrestlers, race-horses, etc.', is perhaps below its high standard in the examples which it offers. In 1774 Goldsmith wrote that 'though the Savages held out and, as the phrase is, had better bottoms, yet for a spurt the Englishmen were more nimble and speedy'. Bewick in 1790 referred to 'what is called in the language of the turf, bottom'. In 1822, Byron was writing '[He] died all game and bottom', and in 1835 the *Penny Cyclopedia* was explaining that horses had 'their manes and tails cropped ... under the supposition that it adds to their strength and bottom'. Patterson wrote of the British troops in 1862: 'For solidity, bottom and courage that never wavers, they are incomparable.' It was a defensive quality. Horace Walpole had it, with his own addition of humour. When one of the houses next door had caught fire, he was wakened in the middle of the night by his valet, whose first words were that he was not to be frightened. 'No, Harry,' said Horace obediently, 'I am not: but what is it that I am not to be frightened at?'

CHAPTER FIVE

Men, Women, and Herveys

THERE was even a small scandal about Horace Walpole himself. It is not mentioned in the Everyman edition of his letters, and Dobson glides over it in a couple of pages, so perhaps it is worth repeating.

He was technically the fourth son of the Prime Minister, in those great days when Ministers controlled places. He was early presented to three fat sinecures which brought him about £2,200 a year, a sum which would be much greater in modern money. He had nothing to do during all his life, except to divert himself or to amuse his friends. He never married. He wrote the letters, and also the first thriller in the English language; he revived the national interest in Gothic architecture, built the phantasy of Strawberry Hill, the 'little Ark with pinnacles', and kept on cramming it with knick-knacks till he died; he had a printing-press of his own, an excellent one; he thrived on gossip, and on playing at loo or at hazard with a duchess or two; when he died, he was eighty, full of years, gout, and honours, for he had succeeded his nephew as the fourth Earl of Orford. The Toynbee edition of sixteen volumes contains 3,061 long letters, of which the following is one of the shortest samples, written to a friend in Jersey:

TO RICHARD BENTLEY, ESQ. Wednesday, June 11, 1755
I was prevented from finishing my letter yesterday, by what do you think? By no less magnificent a circumstance than a deluge. We have had an extraordinary drought, no grass, no leaves, no flowers; not a white rose for the festival of

yesterday! About four arrived such a flood, that we could not see out of the windows: the whole lawn was a lake, though situated on so high an Ararat: presently it broke through the leads, drowned the pretty blue bedchamber, passed through ceilings and floor into the little parlour, terrified Harry, and opened all Catherine's watergates and speech-gates. I had but just time to collect two dogs, a couple of sheep, a pair of bantams, and a brace of gold-fish; for, in the haste of my zeal to imitate my ancestor Noah, I forgot that fish would not easily be drowned. In short, if you chance to spy a little Ark with pinnacles sailing towards Jersey, open the skylight, and you will find some of your acquaintance. You never saw such a desolation! A pigeon brings word that Mabland has fared still worse; it never came into my head before, that a rainbow-office for insuring against water might be very necessary. This is a true account of the late deluge.

Witness our hands,

HORACE NOAH
CATHERINE NOAH, her + mark
HENRY SHEM
LOUIS JAPHET
PETER HAM, &c.

This may be a fair summary of what most people know about Horace Walpole. But the fact which they do not mention in the Everyman edition, is that the great gossip might never have been a son of Sir Robert Walpole's at all.

Lady Louisa Stuart admitted the scandal to print, in her introduction to the letters of her grandmother, Lady Mary Wortley Montagu (1837); but she claimed that it had been a recognized story among people of the 'ton' for many years. Creevey had, indeed, already fastened on it in a letter written in 1833: 'I never knew before that Horace was not the son of Sir Robert Walpole, but of a Lord Hervey, and that Sir Robert knew it and shewed that he did.' Creevey had obtained his information from Lord Holland, and the bulk of Walpole's correspondence was preserved at Holland House, so the suspicion rests on fairly good evidence. To understand it properly, however, we have to know a little about the family of Hervey.

Mankind, Lady Mary Wortley Montagu had said, was divided into Men, Women, and Herveys. She did not mean to imply that the family were perverts by the third category, though less observant people than herself had sometimes been deluded into that idea, by the effeminate appearance, by the eccentric behaviour, and by the cultured occupations of this unusual brood.

We have already met the most famous of them, the Duchess of Marlborough's 'Lady Fanny', Pope's 'Sporus' – John, Lord Hervey.

P. Let Sporus tremble –
                    A. What! that thing of silk?
Sporus! that mere white curd of ass's milk?
Satire or sense, alas! can Sporus feel?
Who breaks a butterfly upon a wheel?
P. Yet let me flap this bug with gilded wings,
This painted child of dirt that stinks and stings!
Whose buzz the witty and the fair annoys;
Yet wit ne'er tastes and beauty ne'er enjoys;
As well-bred spaniels civilly delight
In mumbling of the game they dare not bite.
Eternal smiles his emptiness betray,
As shallow streams run dimpling all the way.
Whether in florid impotence he speaks,
And as the prompter breathes the puppet squeaks;
Or at the ear of Eve, familiar toad!
Half froth half venom spits himself abroad,
In pun or politics, or tales, or lies,
Or spite, or smut, or rhymes, or blasphemies.
His wit all see-saw between that and this,

Now high, now low, now master up, now miss,
And he himself one vile antithesis.
Amphibious thing! that acting either part,
The trifling head or the corrupted heart,
Fop at the toilet, flatterer at the board,
Now trips a lady and now struts a lord.
Eve's tempter thus the rabbins have expressed.
A cherub's face – a reptile all the rest!
Beauty that shocks you, parts that none can trust,
Wit that can creep, and pride that licks the dust!

Yes, but Sporus was the father of eight children. The exact story of Lord Hailes about the ass's milk, which Hervey took because he was a sick man, was that he confined himself to a diet of 'a small quantity of asses' milk and a flour biscuit ... Once a week, he indulged himself with eating an apple; he used emetics daily.' He painted his face with rouge in consequence of this terrible discipline – for the epilepsy from which he believed himself to suffer – 'to soften his ghastly appearance'. Far from tripping it as a lady, he had fought a memorable duel with Pulteney, in which both combatants were wounded.

It was not the only duel in which the clan of Hervey became involved, through the stupidity of their opponents in expecting them to be effeminate. Another instance was George, the eldest son of Sporus, whose imbroglio with the bumpkin Lord Cobham was recorded by Walpole.

About ten days ago, at the new Lady Cobham's assembly, Lord Hervey was leaning over a chair talking to some women, and holding his hat in his hand. Lord Cobham came up and spit in it – yes, spit in it! – and then, with a loud laugh, turned to Nugent, and said, 'Pay me my wager.' In short, he had laid a guinea that he committed this absurd brutality, and that it was not resented. Lord Hervey, with great temper and sensibility, asked if he had any further occasion for his hat? – 'Oh! I see you are angry!' – 'Not very well pleased.' Lord Cobham took the fatal hat, and wiped it, made a thousand apologies, and wanted to pass it off for a joke. Next morning he rose with the sun, and went to visit Lord Hervey; so did Nugent; he would not see them, but wrote to the Spitter (or, as he is now called, Lord Gob'em), to say, that he had affronted him very grossly before company, but having involved Nugent in it, he desired to know to which he was to address himself for satisfaction. Lord Cobham wrote him a most submissive answer, and begged pardon both in his own and Nugent's name. Here it rested for a few days; till getting wind, Lord Hervey wrote again to insist on an explicit apology under Lord Cobham's own hand, with a rehearsal of the excuses that had been made to him. This too was complied with, and the *fair conqueror* shews all the letters.

Another of these Herveys was the Earl-bishop, Earl of Bristol and Bishop of Derry, who went to Dublin dressed 'entirely in purple, with diamond knee- and shoe-buckles, with white gloves fringed with gold lace and fastened with long gold tassels', and who went, incidentally, with strong suspicions among those who welcomed him that, although a bishop, he was not a Christian. Yet another Hervey was the friend of Dr Johnson, Thomas Hervey, who wrote the famous postscript, 'P.S. I am going to part with my wife', and about whose brother Henry the old blunderbuss of Fleet Street said: 'Call a dog Hervey, and I would love him.' Another eccentric was the nautical Hervey who married the notorious Miss Chudleigh with a ring of the bed-curtain. She was the maid-of-honour who had reached the headlines by going to a masquerade in a gauze dress as Iphigenia the Sacrifice, 'but so naked', said Lady Mary Wortley Montagu acidly, 'that the high priest might easily inspect the entrails of the victim'.

This Hervey subsequently abetted her bigamous marriage to the Duke of Kingston, during his own lifetime. A final oddity, John's grandson, used to wear padded waistcoats to fight duels, kept his father tied to a bear, and ended by being hanged. It was of him that an Earl of Lonsdale used to relate the anecdote that 'there was a man who bet a wager he would insult him; so going very near him in a coffee-house, he said – "I smell an Irishman!" to which the other replied – "You shall never smell another!" and, taking up a knife, cut off his nose.'

The Herveys, then, were at least peculiar. They also wrote poetry and history, liked music, paid attention to architecture, did unusual things, were beyond the comprehension of ordinary bullies like Cobham, and had a family likeness in the face.

Horace Walpole had the Hervey face, which was unmistakable. 'No beings in human shape,' said Lady Louisa Stuart, 'could resemble each other less than the two passing for father and son.' 'In every respect,' said Cunningham, 'he was unlike a Walpole, and in every respect, figure and formation of mind, very like a Hervey.' This has a special meaning, when one remembers Lady Mary Wortley Montagu's division of the human race: it means that Horry resembled something singular.

And then there was his own description of the Norfolk Walpoles, to whom he believed himself to belong:

I shudder when I see them brandish their knives in act to carve, and look on them as savages that devour one another. I should not stare at all more than I do, if yonder Alderman at the lower end of the table was to stick his fork into his neighbour's jolly cheek, and cut a brave slice of brown and fat. Why, I'll swear I see no difference between a country gentleman and a sirloin; whenever the first laughs, or the latter is cut, there run out just the same streams of gravy!'

Sir Robert, the official father, was such a person. He was startlingly fat – '*avec ce gros corps*' said the Queen, '*ces jambes enflées, et ce vilain ventre*' – vulgar in his jokes – always talked bawdry at table, according to Boswell, so that everybody could join in – a good farmer-like statesman and foxhunter, who opened his gamekeeper's letters first and who might have made an equal fortune as a cattle-dealer. His motto was: *Quieta non movere*: Leave well alone – just the motto for a husband whose wife may have been unfaithful.

This brings the scandal to its evidence.

Catherine Shorter, Sir Robert Walpole's first wife, had five children. Four of them were born in a sequence after the marriage; the fifth, Horace, was born eleven years later, at a time when she was known to be on bad terms with Sir Robert, and known to be on romantic terms with Carr, Lord Hervey, an elder half-brother of Pope's Sporus. Carr himself died young and unmarried, when Horace was six, so we lack his version of the story.

On reviewing these points, it may seem possible that Horry, as he was called by his familiars (behind his back), was a Hervey rather than a Walpole. He did the Hervey things. He built Strawberry just as the Earl-bishop built Downhill. He enjoyed the arts of literature and history like Sporus, arts which seemed contemptible to the Norfolk sirloins of Sir Robert's race. He was effeminate. He ran on the tips of his toes, they said, like a peewit. He was devoted to gossip, 'at the ear of Eve', like Queen Caroline's pet. Perhaps the best account of him was by Laetitia Matilda Hawkins:

His entrance into a room was in that style of affected delicacy, which fashion had made almost natural, *chapeau bras* between his hands as if he wished to compress it, or under his arm; knees bent, and feet on tip-toe, as if afraid of a wet floor. His summer dress of ceremony was usually a lavender suit, the waistcoat embroidered with a little silver, or of white silk worked in the tambour, partridge silk stockings, gold buckles, ruffles and lace frill. In the winter he wore powder ... His appearance at the breakfast table was proclaimed, and attended, by a fat and favourite little dog, the legacy of Madame du Deffand; the dog and a favourite squirrel partook of his breakfast. He generally dined at four ... His dinner when at home was of chicken, pheasant, or any light food, of which he ate sparingly. Pastry he disliked, as difficult of digestion, though he would taste a morsel of venison pie. Iced water, then a London dislike, was his favourite drink. The scent of dinner was removed by a censer or pot of frankincense. The wine that was drunk was drunk during dinner. After his coffee he would take a pinch of snuff, and nothing more that night.

Pope was a malevolent cripple, not noted for telling the truth. If we winnow the venom from his picture of Sporus, there does seem to remain a family resemblance between that picture and Miss Hawkins's. Sporus, like Horace, was abstemious and sparely built – Horace boasts of his own 'no-weight', saying that he cannot hurt himself by falling downstairs. Silk dresses naturally figure on both canvases, but in both cases the artist found them special enough to mention, in an age of such costume. Sporus trips like a lady, Horace like a peewit, or as if the floor were wet. Sporus goes in for politics, tales, spite, and rhymes: so did Horace. Sporus has a 'trifling head', Horace trifles with the bric-à-brac of Strawberry. Both men are fastidious. Sporus is a fop at the toilet, and Horace has a pot of frankincense to take away the smell of dinner.

In another respect they were similar, for Walpole had the Hervey courage. When the Gordon Riots took place, he went to London at the age of sixty-three, to be in them.

I could not bear to sit here in shameful selfish philosophy, and hear the millions of reports, and know almost all I loved in danger, without sharing it. I went to town on Wednesday, and though the night was the most horrible I ever beheld, I would not take millions not to have been present. . . . I drove from one place to another till two, but did not get to bed till between three and four. . . . I have so much exerted my no-strength, and had so little sleep these two nights, that I came hither today for some rest.

When he was attacked by highwaymen, as he was twice, and once dangerously, he behaved with sang-froid.

Voici le fait. Lady Browne and I were, as usual, going to the Duchess of Montrose at seven o'clock. The evening was very dark. In the close lane under her park pale, within twenty yards of her gate, a black figure on horseback pushed by between the chaise and the hedge on my side. I suspected it was a highwayman, and so I found did Lady Browne, for she was speaking and dropped. To divert her fears, I was just going to say, Is not that the apothecary going to the Duchess? when I heard a voice cry 'Stop!' and the figure came back to the chaise. I had the presence of mind, before I let down the glass, to take out my watch and stuff it within my waistcoat under my arm. He said, 'Your purses and watches!' I replied, 'I have no watch.' 'Then your purse!' I gave it to him; it had nine guineas. It was so dark that I could not see his hand, but felt him take it. He then asked for Lady Browne's purse, and said, 'Don't be frightened; I will not hurt you.' I said, 'No; you won't frighten the lady?' He replied, 'No; I give you my word I will do you no hurt.' Lady Browne gave him her purse, and was going to add her watch, but he said, 'I am much obliged to you! I wish you good night!' pulled off his hat, and rode away. 'Well,' said I, 'Lady Browne, you will not be afraid of being robbed another time, for you see there is nothing in it.'

Both Walpole and Hervey were people of masculine judgement. It is a mistake to think of the former as a dear old gentleman. On the contrary, both were as sharp as Voltaire, and not much easier to get on with. Hervey was the kind of person who could refuse to claim that his own memoirs were not partial, 'since whoever is so must always be it, either without knowing or without owning it'. Walpole was the kind of person who said of his own works – the *Castle of Otranto*, the *Mysterious Mother*, *Anecdotes of Painting*, *Noble Authors*, *Historic Doubts*, etc. – with penetration, humility, and apparent sincerity:

I have learnt and practised the humiliating task of comparing myself with great authors; and that comparison has annihilated all the flattery that self-love could suggest. I know how trifling my own writings are, and how far below the standard that constitutes excellence. ... My simple writings have had better fortune than they had any reason to expect; and I fairly believe, in a great degree, because gentlemen-writers ... are treated with some civility if they do not write absolute nonsense.

There is a point which may be of interest to the biologist, if the irregular parentage should be assumed. It may be of interest that the hereditary tendencies of separate people should have expressed themselves in an identical way, each without the knowledge of the other. For both Hervey and Walpole wrote memoirs of the court, without showing them to each other, and these memoirs were inseparable in tone and content.

On the one hand, then, there was the Hervey family, polished, abstemious, and light of bone like birds. Particularly there was Sporus, the younger brother of

Horace's putative father, Carr – 'whose early death', as Pope said of the latter, 'deprived the family of as much wit and honour as he left behind in any part of it'. On the other hand there was the Rowlandson figure of the Prime Minister, so gross that he could hardly stand and who had to be accommodated with a chair when talking to the Queen – then a rare distinction – good natured, able at figures – which Horace never could understand – and described by Lord Chesterfield as 'inelegant in his manners . . . loose in his morals . . . with a strong, coarse wit, which he was too free of for a man in his station, as it is always inconsistent with dignity'. Between them stood Horace, 'the most eccentric', according to the pettish Macaulay, 'the most artificial, the most fastidious, the most capricious of mortals – his mind a bundle of inconsistent whims and affectations – his features covered with mask within mask, which, when the outer disguise of obvious affectation was removed, you were still as far as ever from seeing the real man'. It is interesting to compare Macaulay on Walpole with Pope on Hervey.

It can make no difference to the devotees of Horry, which of them the father really was, except if it throws any light on his own character. We must be content to be indebted to the one or to the other. It does throw some light, however, for he always treated the official father, Sir Robert, with the deepest gratitude: either because he was grateful for not being treated as a bastard, or else because he wanted to emphasize that he was not a bastard, or else because he was not.

In this connexion, there is a point for the psychiatrist. The unconscious mind of Horace once produced a quotation so stunningly apposite, and qualified it so carefully, that it seems to be worth consideration. He was discussing the pleasures of retirement from parliamentary business, when he wrote in one of his letters:

For my part, I say with the Bastard in King John, – though with a little more reverence, and only as touching his ambition, –

'Oh, old Sir Robert, father, on my knee
I give Heaven thanks I was not like to thee.'

Such is the evidence about paternity, for what it is worth: but the importance of the doyen of the Age of Scandal lay in his life, not in his birth. It was an enviable life, and he himself had possessed the sense, as well as the opportunity, to make it so.

Horace Walpole used to get up late. He would breakfast with the dogs and squirrel, then dress himself and saunter in the gardens of Strawberry, where he would direct the operations of his builders and plasterers, play with Tonton or Patapan, and arrange whatever printing or gilding he happened to have on hand. At twelve o'clock a 'light-bodied chariot' would be at the door, with his coachman and valet, and he would drive to London before dinner, to see if there was any news upon the wing. Returned to Strawberry, he would find his dinner waiting at the unfashionable hour of four o'clock. 'I am,' he wrote in 1789, 'so antiquated as still to dine at four, though frequently prevented, as many are so good as to call on me at that hour, because it is too soon for them to go home and dress so early in the morning.' After dinner, or perhaps before it, he might have put on his 'dress of ceremony', which might now be called his evening dress. The difference between the two costumes is illustrated by the most delightful of his vulgar stories.

You will be diverted with what happened to Mr Meynell lately. He was engaged to dine at a formal old lady's, but stayed so late hunting that he had not time to dress, but went as he was, with forty apologies. The matron very affected, and meaning to say something very civil, cried, 'Oh! Sir, I assure you I can see the gentleman through a pair of buckskin breeches as well as if he were in silk or satin.'

Once Horry was in the full fig, he would set out for his evening call, some visit to a Birthday or to a Drawing-room, or perhaps to play at hazard in the 'family' of one of the dowager princesses. When he had returned from this, or if he had stayed at home for the night, he would sit down to write at ten o'clock, taking several cups of coffee while he worked. There, in the Blue Room or the Library, he would 'write letters of news to Mann or Montagu, acknowledge cards of invitation from peers or peeresses, give life to the antiquarian notes of Vertue the engraver, paste Fairthornes and Hollars into his volumes of English heads, annotate a favourite author, and retire to rest about two in the morning'.

The villa of Strawberry Hill, which he created, has been subjected to a certain amount of ill-natured fun, and, it might be added, to ill-informed fun, by the pomposity of architects. They say that it was not true Gothic, but bastard and degenerate. Walpole was one of the first people who paid attention to 'Gothick' architecture at all; it was not to be expected that he would understand its principles from the start. Nor did he intend the house to be taken seriously. It was a fantasy, half a joke: a fairy story in lath and plaster which he called into being like the décor of a Russian ballet: and he himself was the first to be aware of its insolemnity. When the famous printing-press had given birth to a copy of polite verses for the visiting nobility, he would make 'a private signal', and French horns and clarinets would accompany the compliment from the

95

lawn. French visitors complained that it was not '*digne de la solidité anglaise*'. He was always threatening to wrap it up, it was so small, and to enclose it in the letter he was writing. 'It was built,' he said, 'to please my own taste and in some degree to realize my own visions.' In the end he wrote pathetically of his 'poor little Strawberry', since so prophetically: 'My buildings are paper, like my writings, and both will be blown away in ten years after I am dead.'

We know every room in Strawberry Hill [said Cunningham in 1858, after all the ornaments had been auctioned and when nothing remained except the descriptions in the letters or the catalogue] and every miniature and full-length portrait in the Tribune and Gallery. We are admitted to the Holbein chamber and the Beauclerk closet, and as we wander in print over the stripped rooms and now new furnished walls, we can pass a night in his favourite Blue Room, restore the Roman Eagle, replace the bust of Vespasian and the armour of Francis I; bring back from Knowsley the blue and white china bowl, commemorated in the Odes of Gray, and call up Kirgate, the printer, carrying a proof of the 'Anecdotes of Painting' to Conway's 'Elzevir Horace' in the Gothic Library. As we become better acquainted with his letters, we can summon before us the skilful antiquary and virtuoso midwife, and see Strawberry in lilac-tide – that period of the year in which its owner thought Strawberry in perfection.

CHAPTER SIX

Sporus

JOHN, LORD HERVEY, was born in 1696, long before the Age of Scandal.

He belonged to a singular family, and had the singular fate to become the hero of the most vituperative verses in the English language. It was not difficult to be an enemy of Pope's. Hervey's father was a charming person, who, in spite of political differences, remained on loving terms with his son, only complaining bitterly about the young man's addiction to tea – 'that detestable and poisonous plant, which had once brought him to death's door, and if persisted in would carry him through it'. His wife, Mary Lepell, a bold and noted belle who had been the toast of the town, and who had been considered by the Duchess of Marlborough to be 'extreme forward and pert', loved him faithfully, and bore him eight children. Lady Mary Wortley Montagu was a friend till death. The Queen admitted him to her bed-chamber, creating a precedent in this, calling him her 'child' and saying: 'It is well I am so old, or I should be talked of for this creature.' Princess Caroline loved him vainly. The King trusted him; and so did Sir Robert Walpole, the shrewdest of men.

Hervey was born in Suffolk, the eldest son of the first Earl of Bristol. He went to Westminster and Cambridge, then to France before he was twenty, thence to Hanover, and then home to Ickworth to pass his time in 'the perpetual pursuit of poetry'. He married at twenty-four, and became attached to the court of the

Prince of Wales, who was to become King George II. It is notable that this was his first attachment. In later years, he was to be false to Pulteney or to Sir Robert Walpole, accordingly as these people fell out with Caroline and her husband, but he remained faithful to his *milieu*, which was the court. His was a personal attachment to the future Queen.

He entered the House of Commons at twenty-nine, joining Pulteney against Walpole. When 'dapper George' had succeeded, and had adopted Walpole, against expectation, Hervey left Pulteney and followed Walpole. He had never been a servant of Pulteney's, as he never was one of Walpole's. He went with the new King and Queen as before, and not for reasons of preferment.

After a visit to Italy with Stephen Fox, he became involved in a duel with Pulteney, which was fought because of the dedication to a political pamphlet. He would have been killed, except that Pulteney's foot slipped, and both combatants were wounded.

Hervey was Caroline's pet, and rendered service to Sir Robert Walpole while they were in alliance – by smoothing difficulties through the back stairs. This was his essential occupation: to help the court, and to help those who happened to be in favour with the court, by the offices of liaison. He was an early and unbribed example of the 'King's Friend', as established in the next reign. Already Vice-Chamberlain of the Household and a member of the Privy Council, he was appointed Lord Privy Seal at the age of forty-four.

His ally Walpole resigned in 1741, and Hervey continued to adhere to his real master, the King, provoking Horry Walpole to bitter remarks, dictated by the filial allegiance of the latter to Sir Robert. Hervey, he said,

was 'too ill to go to the operas, yet, with a coffin face,
is as full of his little dirty politics as ever'.

He adhered until he was dismissed – for the Queen
had died in 1737 and thus removed his *raison d'être* –
then went into opposition, began to fail himself, and
died at the age of forty-six in 1743.

As politicians went, this was a history of fidelity.
Hervey was not a place-hunter, but a neighbouring
friend who had become attracted to the royal family
in the gossiping way. It was for this that the Queen had
valued him. He had amused her, and he had known
that he did so, and he had been pleased that this should
be. He had been sorry for the woman, in her strange
predicament of royalty, and he had tried to ease its
burden.

His own burdens had not been light. The story of
Lord Hailes, that he lived on one biscuit a day, with a
little ass's milk and an apple a week, taking emetics
daily, was exaggerated or confined to a brief interlude.
He himself wrote to his doctor in 1732:

To let you know that I continue one of your most pious
votaries, and to tell you the method I am in. In the first
place, I never take wine nor malt drink, or any liquid but
water and milk-tea; in the next, I eat no meat but the
whitest, youngest, and tenderest, nine times in ten nothing
but chicken, and never more than the quantity of a small
one at a meal. I seldom eat any supper, but if any, nothing
absolutely but bread and water; two days in the week I eat
no flesh; my breakfast is dry biscuit not sweet, and green
tea; I have left off butter as bilious; I eat no salt, nor any
sauce but bread sauce. I take a Scotch pill once a week, and
thirty grains of Indian root when my stomach is loaded, my
head giddy, and my appetite gone. I have not bragged of
the persecutions I suffer in this cause; but the attacks made
on me by ignorance, impertinence, and gluttony are
innumerable and incredible.

'Beef?' he was supposed to have said once, possibly under one of these attacks by ignorant gluttons. 'Oh, no! Faugh! Don't you know I never eat beef, nor *horse*, nor any of those things?'

He seems to have thought of his disease as epilepsy, though it might have been an unbalanced diet and the green tea of which his father complained, or perhaps one of the toxic conditions so common in his century. He wrote to Stephen Fox:

I have been so very much out of order since I writ last, that going into the Drawing Room before the King, I was taken with one of those disorders with the odious name, that you know happen'd to me once at Lincoln's Inn Fields playhouse. I had just warning enough to catch hold of somebody (God knows who) in one side of the lane made for the King to pass through, and stopped till he was gone by. I recovered my senses enough immediately to say, when people came up to me asking what was the matter, that it was a *cramp* took me suddenly in my leg, and (that *cramp* excepted) that I was as well as ever I was in my life. I was far from it; for I saw everything in a mist, was so giddy I could hardly walk, which I said was owing to my *cramp* not quite gone off. To avoid giving suspicion I stayed and talked with people about ten minutes, and then (the Duke of Grafton being there to light the King) came down to my lodgings, where + + +. I am now far from well, but better, and pro-digiously pleased, since I was to feel this disorder, that I contrived to do it *à l'insu de tout le monde*. Mr Churchill was close by me when it happened, and takes it all for a *cramp*. The King, Queen, &c., inquired about my *cramp* this morning, and laughed at it; I joined in the laugh, said how foolish an accident it was, and so it has passed off; nobody but Lady Hervey (from whom it was impossible to conceal what followed) knows anything of it.

Whatever it was, the disorder was real, as his early death showed. Pope's wicked jeers about the ass's milk, or about Narcissus who 'look'd a white lily sunk beneath a shower'; the Duchess of Marlborough's sneers from the same poet about 'Lady Fanny'; even Horry's squibs at the 'coffin face' and the common titter raised about the rouge with which he tried to colour the lily, must seem distressing against these facts. He had a pointed face, said the implacable Duchess, and not a tooth in his head. She did not mention, nor perceive, the courage with which he had faced these disabilities, nor the sensitiveness with which he had tried to hide them.

When he was dying, he wrote to Lady Mary Wortley Montagu:

I have been confined these three weeks with a fever, which is a sort of annual tax my detestable constitution pays to our detestable climate at the return of every spring; it is now much abated, though not quite gone off . . . Adieu! my head is still so weak that it turns round with what I have written. I will write again when I grow stronger. The public affairs are in a strange posture; and I believe you know as much of them where you are, and what we would be at, as any minister in the cabinet. I am sure I know no more than if I had been born an idiot.

Finally, in his last letter, of which the handwriting quavered as it went, he distilled the pessimism of a dying Roman:

The last stages of an infirm life are filthy roads, and like all other roads I find the farther one goes from the capital the more tedious the miles grow and the more rough and disagreeable the way. I know of no turnpikes to mend them; medicine pretends to be such, but doctors who have the management of it, like the commissioners for most other turnpikes, seldom execute what they undertake: they only put the toll of the poor cheated passenger in their pockets, and leave every jolt at least as bad as they found it, if not worse. 'May all your ways (as Solomon says of wisdom) be ways of pleasantness, and all your paths peace'; and when your dissolution must come, may it be like that of your lucky workman. Adieu!

The 'lucky workman' had died young and suddenly, by falling from a builder's scaffold.

'But let me flap,' Pope had said, 'this bug with gilded wings, this painted child of dirt....' Hervey had been a butterfly, as Pope perceived, and as Beau Brummell was later to seek to be. But he had been a butterfly of cynicism and reservation. Dismissed from the court which he had always served, and writing his memoirs as a dying man, he retained an unemotional disdain. He looked, as he wrote, at Caroline the Queen who had liked him, as a lepidopterist might look at the moth which he was setting. It was the scientific, the noble attitude. Even to the Queen's daughter, the Princess Caroline, who had died in love with him, he accorded only the politeness of silence. And to Pope's odious personalities about Sporus, he had replied, with the aid of Lady Mary Wortley Montagu:

If none with vengeance yet thy crimes pursue,
Or give thy manifold deserts their due:
If limbs unbroken, skin without a stain,
Unwhip't, unblanketed, unkick'd, unslain,
That wretched little carcase you retain,
The reason is, not that the world wants eyes,
But thou'rt too mean, they see, and they despise.

Lord Hervey was one of those people about whom it was difficult to be moderate. If hated, as he was by Pope, he was bound to be hated excessively. If loved, a *hysterica passio* rises against his detractors. He was, in literature, as dispassionate as Pavlov with his unfortunate dogs. He had the Roman fashion, which refused to pity or to distort. At the same time, perhaps for relief from these altitudes, he was a lap-dog who amused himself with tattle. It was, in the main, the Spartan attitude. What was the value of life? He was ill and rich and growing old: the *Dictionary of National Biography* might come to talk of his 'continued infidelities': but he had one criterion unblemished, the devotion to truth so far as he was able to perceive it, and, after that, he was content to amuse a dilettante Queen, with the butterfly gossip of an unbelieving age.

CHAPTER SEVEN

The Mob

THE elegance of the sedan chair, however, ought not to lead us into overlooking the grimy faces of those who often peered through its glasses, or spattered it with mud in a riot, or died on foreign battlefields to preserve the comforts of its patrician owner. It is an astonishing fact that the dilettante and romantic period of Horace Walpole should have also been the period which brought England to the temporary leadership of the world, and that the generations which bred the owner of Strawberry should also have been breeding the victors of Trafalgar and Waterloo. Walpole was born within sound of Blenheim, Ramillies, Oudenarde, and Malplaquet, lived through Dettingen, Fontenoy, and Minden, and heard of Napoleon's victory at Lodi before he died. He saw America made and lost, India and Canada added, the broad lines of the British Empire laid down. Nelson was thirty-nine at Walpole's death, Wellington twenty-eight. It was scarcely an era of peaceful decadence, when the letter-writer could observe, in allusion to an assassination committed by the Empress Catherine:

Queen of Hungary, debtor to the human species.

Millions.
King of Prussia, ditto...............................
do.
King of France, by his stewards.....................
do.

King of Spain..

Many thousands, ditto.

Prince Ferdinand, a private gentleman................

Some thousands.

Czarina...

Only her own husband.

Total   Half Europe.

The debts of the species were paid by the inarticulate plebs, and their snail's-eye view of England's glory was largely without historians. One witness survived, however, in the Orrery Papers, a yeoman of cavalry who wrote home to his village, to say that he was safe, when George II had done with flourishing his sword at Dettingen – to the amusement of Frederick the Great and to the edification of courtly annalists.

To MR THOS. STILMAN. IN FROOM IN SOMERSETSHIR IN ENGLAND. THUS:

Dear Brother, – I send you thes Lins to Let you know that i am in good helth and now i can with plether send you the happy nus of ouer Suckses in the Batel that hapened the 15 of this Month and now i shal proceed with the perteklers which was as folos thusday in the morning at 5 a Clock the french begun playing thar Cannon upon ouer Baggeg from a batery thay had raisd at the other sid the Main and so continued tel 20 Minuets after 8 and then thay turned thar Cannon upon us and all our rogmonts of hors and Draggouns tel 12 which you may think it strang but is hall tel you the Cos of it thay had got 40 Thousand in a wood Just a gainst ouer right whing in order as soun as we was marcht up to fall in upon ouer rear and so we should ben confined in frunt and rear with the water at one side of us and a wood at the other but it was happyly discouered and ouer Cannon set brisk to Work and by 12 lat the wood about thar ears and Drof them to the rest of the Army and then we marcht up all the foot in the frunt of ouer right Whing and the Draggouns in the Center and all the hors upon the left and his Magisty in the front of the old Bufs as bold as a liont with his can in one hand and his Sord in the other. So when thay cam up to them we all gav three housays and all the futt gave 3 the mortels chers that euer was known and the french turned tail and run to the water side in hops of gitting ouer thar brige but while we cape them in play the queins men puld doun the brige and a bout 2 thousand of them was fos into the water so that the Main is be com a Seckent Denuap so then ouer Lift whing cam into play and ouer regmont pusht in upon the gandarins which is the french Life gards and a regmont of Dragguns and the first pus has we mad Mr Vizard was at my rite hand so we had ouer Sords upon ouer rist and ouer pistols in ouer hand and before Mr Vizard could droy his triger his hors was shot and ded upon the Spot and Vizard's legg laid under one horses belly i dropt my pistol and i hold out my Sord with a stif arm and cot the blos and neuer waged tel i so Mr Viz Leg clear of his hors so he got of clear with only the Lost of his bags and Shurts and all the things that he had it was a mortel hot batel as euer was seain in this aeige as i haf heard ofescers say sence god knos i thote euery minuet to be my Last. for i thote that all of them presented at me and the whirling of the bols mad me all most dif butt god allmity heard my prars and brot me clear without anny woond when i was in hottes of the battell i was so past fear Mr Figors hors was shot and Mr Gorgs hors and Mr Meeis had his belt cut of in to but did him no harm dockter Hatthon is shot through the body and stil alife and like to do well the most shocking thing was to hear the cris of the wooned french as we rid over when we prsud them but we could not help it so when the batel was ouer which was about 7 a clock we marcht to a plas to in camp on and then 4 Men of a trop was orderd to goe back to tak up ouer tents and citels and all the rest of ouer camp Mitterils and i was one of them and then my hart was shoked mos of all for mos a mile to gether my hors could not step for ded men and horses we lost 15

hundred Men and some ods beside woonded and the french
Lost 9 thousand beside woonded the 26 all the whole army
fired 3 times after prars for Joy of Vicktory i was upon the
vangard for a fortnight be for the battel and i thought it
hard work but no thing is so hard as kiling of Men pray
my Dear Brother giue my Deuty to my Dear wife and
Children and my love to my Brothers and Sisters and all my
relations and all that do ax for me it is my dayly prars to
god that i may life to com home and lif in happness with
my Dear Wife and Children which is all at present from
your most loveing Brother   EDWARD STILMAN

i mad what in queery i can and sent Jams numan to all the
regmonts that he could go to find out if thar was anny of
my tounsmen ded and he could find but one which was
Thomas Wilkons his head was shot of by a cannon bal the
regmont that Samul pew belong to is 5 Mils from ouers so i
got Liberti and rid to him and i found him in good helth i
could not stay with him not abofe 5 minuts he givs his
Deauty to his wife and his love to all pray send to in gineral
Hunywood's regmont near Ashaffingburg or els whar.

'No thing is so hard as kiling of Men.' The truth of
this aphorism, and the dread of the 'whirling of the
bols': these were no secret to the generals who arranged
the slaughter. It was Frederick's policy to keep his infantry at the sticking point by making them more afraid
of their officers than of the enemy, and the private
soldier who marched up Bunker's Hill in haversack and
great-coat, to be blown away by volley after volley, was
known in America as a 'lobster' or 'bloody back', because of his red coat and the crimson on his naked
shoulders when he was flogged. Even the champions of
freedom who awaited him at the top of the hill were
learning to be regulars. 'Every one is made to know his
place,' wrote a chaplain of Washington's army, 'and
keep it, or be tied up and receive thirty or forty lashes
according to his crime.' So unsuitable to the American

climate was the formal uniform of the British soldier, amounting to a 'livery' with its leather stock, that three sergeants and fifty-six men fell dead of heat at Monmouth Court House, without a wound. George the King carried a cane, for his own troops, as well as a sword for the enemy. One of his soldiers claimed to have received in all 30,000 lashes, 'yet the man is hearty and well and in no ways concerned'.

Discipline was draconic. The mercenaries hired out by the Landgrave of Hesse Cassel were attended by an executioner and his assistants as part of the establishment; and the phrase 'as bold as a liont', with which Edward Stilman had described his sovereign, happened also to be applied by Thicknesse to an old soldier placed before the firing squad.

A general court martial upon a sergeant for such a crime, implied death upon the first face of it, and as I had been informed that the prisoner bore a good character, and that his desertion was owing to his possessing an unusual share of sentiment, I attended his tryal. The charge being read to the prisoner, he was asked whether he pleaded guilty or innocent? to which the brave man replied, guilty to be sure; it would be impertinent in me to trifle with your honours by denying it. Then what have you to say, asked the president, before the sentence of death is passed upon you? to the best of my remembrance the following noble, but alas! fruitless defence was made. – Gentlemen, said this SENTIMENTAL SOLDIER, I was in a manner born a soldier, my father was a soldier before me, and I have been all my days, as it were of the same profession, and since I have been a sergeant, I appeal to my captain, and the officers of the company to which I belong, how I have acquitted myself, but as I did not associate so much with the private men, as other sergeants do, in order the better to support my own authority, or to carry the orders of your honours into execution, I was rather disliked by the rank and file-men, and as my wife had been accused (whether guilty or innocent I cannot say) of stealing a handkerchief, the men when I was doing my own duty, or obeying the orders of your honours, were continually calling out from every corner of the garrison, *Hep* – whose wife stole the handkerchief? – whose wife stole the handkerchief? And this insult being daily and constantly repeated, it so overcome me with wretchedness, and misery of mind, that in a fit of despair, I took the fatal resolution of going off, which I could have done with the company's money, to whom I was master pay sergeant, since which, I have been a miserable wanderer, and almost starved, for I knew not how, or where to get my bread but in that line of life to which I had been accustomed, this is the truth gentlemen, and I submit my case to your honours consideration, in hopes that my life will be spared, and my future services useful, the man was condemned to be shot to death! ! when the fatal day of his execution arrived, I chose he should not die under my *immediate* command, and therefore quitted the garrison, desiring an old trusty sensible invalid soldier, for whom I had much good will, to attend the execution and let me know *every particular*, that passed at it. He promised so to do, but not without assuring me, he would not have seen such a *deadly blow*, if I had not desired it. Upon my asking him how the old sergeant behaved? he replied, sir, he went out as bold as a lion; but recollecting, that by saying so, I might conceive him to have gone out with an hardened unbecoming boldness, he recalled those words, and said, he died sir like a MAN: observing that the prisoner was the *only* man present who did not tremble! what said I, did Major Debrisay tremble? yes they all trembled, Major, officers and men. The Major then asked the prisoner whether he acknowledged the justice of his sentence? the prisoner said he did: have you then anything to say previous to its being put into execution? yes: – he had a small favour to ask of his honour, and it was, that his fellow prisoner, whom he had just left in the black hold, for a trifling offence, might be forgiven and released? he was promised a compliance to his request, and then, after refusing to have a cap put over his eyes, but to face his hard fate, he was shot to death, according to his sentence. The body was buried in the warren, a spot to which my old invalid, who was my trusty warrener also, and I often visited. After it had lain there seven years, we two, took an early hour, to dig up his bones, as I was determined to preserve the skull of a man, which possessed better brains, than a majority of his court martial members. Upon turning the lid of the coffin over, I was exceedingly surprised, to find the skeleton, blanched as white as snow, by the salt lands and lying in the most perfect order, of a perfect skeleton but with the back turned upwards! I then observed to the old soldier, that the man had been buried before he was quite dead, and had turned himself in the coffin. This for a while staggered my chum's recollection also, but at length he accounted for it, by observing, that the Major had ordered him to lie buried, face downwards, as an additional mark of infamy!

Such was the stuff from which the Thomas Atkins of a later age developed, such the 'article' to which the Iron Duke referred in Brussels, before the battle of Waterloo:

'Do you reckon,' I asked, 'upon any support from the French King's troops at Alost?' – 'Oh!' said he, 'don't mention such fellows! No: I think Blucher and I can do the business.' – Then, seeing a private soldier of one of our infantry regiments enter the park, gaping about at the statues and images: – 'There,' he said, pointing at the soldier, 'it all depends upon that article whether we can do the business or not. Give me enough of it, and I am sure.'

CREEVEY

The situation of the naval rating, recruited perhaps by a press-gang and regarded by his captain as a representative of the 'bêtes, badauds, and black-guards' which was Lord Auckland's description of the proletariat ('Falstaff's men,' said Captain Moore

affectionately in 1803, 'decayed tapsters . . . I am already
inclined to love them. . . . If they fight, I shall worship
them') disciplined with a cat-o'-nine-tails and nour-
ished upon salt pork and grog, paid at the time of the
Nore mutiny only one-quarter of the money commanded by a merchant seaman, valued at the same
price as one vote in an election, expected since the
execution of Admiral Byng to die rather than fail to do,
and possibly agreeing with Dr Johnson that 'no man
will be a sailor, who has contrivance enough to get himself into a jail; for being in a ship is being in a jail, with
the chance of being drowned' – the situation of the
simple heart-of-oak was not of such a kind as would
encourage his self-expression in literature. The voices
which have survived from the lower deck are as rare as
the voices from the barrack square. One voice, like
Edward Stilman's, remains among the pages of
Heneage Jesse's *George the Third*:

There is extant, for instance, among the Mitchell MSS. in
the British Museum, a letter superscribed, – 'For his
Present Mayjesty King George ye third, London', in which
the writer, an English sailor, states that in the month of
May 1766, while enjoying himself on shore near Memel, he
was kidnapped and enlisted against his will into the
Prussian military service. Four times over, he informs the
King, he has represented his hard case to 'his Mayjisty
King of Prows in Berlien', but no notice having been taken
of his letters, he now, by the advice of a 'verry honorowble
ould gentleman, a marchant from Ingland', ventured to
address 'tow or three lines' to his own Sovereign. 'This
letter,' the writer concludes, 'i must smugle away in toan
inglishmans hands that none of the Offiscears catsh me with
this letter. iam 28 years of agge and 5 foot aleaven in hight,
and so no more at prescent, but remain, in prays to the
Allmighty for your Mayjesty's long rean, and in peace with
all men.   JAMES RICHARDSON

From the revow in camps
in Cenesborough May the 31th 1767.

Long as is the letter, from which the foregoing is an extract, and difficult as it is to read from the badness of the writing as well as of the spelling, the King nevertheless not only took the trouble to decipher it, but ordered an immediate investigation into the truth of the statements which it contained. 'His majesty,' writes one of the Secretaries of State, General Conway, to the British Ambassador at Berlin, 'had received a letter by the Post from one James Richardson, an English Sailor, who, above a twelvemonth ago was, partly by force and partly by terror, enlisted in the Prussian service. As the King's disposition inclines him to lend an ear to the complaints of the meanest of his subjects, he perused this letter with attention; and finding in it a remarkable air of truth and sincerity, he directed me to transmit it to you, that you may inquire concerning its grounds and foundation. If the poor man's narrative be found conformable to fact, and if he be enlisted otherwise than from his free choice, it is his Majesty's pleasure that you make application in his behalf to the King of Prussia, and recover him his liberty.' The man's story proved to be correct, and accordingly, within six weeks from the date of General Conway's letter, he obtained his discharge. The following is a copy of Richardson's certificate of his release: –

'This is to sertify that I James Richardson hath got my discharge from lallenboun ridgiment on foot, and hath got one dallar to bear my expences on my way, and a pass, to make the best of my way to owld ingland.

Rassllinbourg September 18th 1767.'

So rare and splendid an intervention must have seemed to James Richardson a miracle. It was the poor 'dallar' which they gave him, the enlistment 'by terror', and the necessity to 'smugle' his letter for fear of the officers, which threw more light upon the circumstances of the period than the good King's glorious behaviour. As Richardson balanced Stilman, so it would be possible to find a pair for the executed sergeant of Governor Thicknesse in the fate of the unfortunate Byng; for all ranks shared in the rigours of the day.

In 1797, when reefing topsails, a Captain Pigot of the *Mermione* called to the men on the mizen-topsail yard that he would flog the last man down. Two of the poor devils, in their hurry to escape the promised flogging, fell to the quarter deck and were killed. 'Throw the lubbers overboard,' said the captain. 'The master of a slave ship, called the "Zong",' says Lecky, 'finding sickness raging among his negroes, deliberately ordered 132 of them to be flung into the sea.' It scarcely comes as a surprise to find that when Thomas Paine, the author of *The Rights of Man*, had joined a privateer in 1753, her name should have been the *Terrible*, and that her commander should have been Captain Death. Stories even more ghastly are to be found in the *Dictionary of National Biography*:

DAVIDSON, WILLIAM (1756?–1795?), privateersman, a native of Scotland, born about 1756, was in 1791 serving as an able seaman on board H.M.S. Niger, then commanded by Sir Richard Keats. Davidson was noted as a comparatively well-educated man of gloomy and silent disposition, but liable to sudden outbursts of temper. While the ship was at Deal he was condemned to be flogged for some such outburst. The punishment caused him excessive agony, and at the fifth stroke he fell into convulsions. The sentence was then remitted, but some time after he struck an officer and was again condemned. While being brought to the gangway he attempted to cut his throat, and this failing, he tried, but also in vain, to throw himself overboard. His punishment was not proceeded with, but he was ordered into confinement. The whole circumstances of the case led to an inquiry into Davidson's past life, and a rumour was found current in the ship that he possessed a journal giving an account of singular atrocities in which he had been engaged.

Davidson's chest was ransacked, the journal was found, and laid before the officers. It narrated that the author on 1 Dec. 1788 had enlisted on board the Saint Dinnan, a Russian privateer, which on 3 Dec. cleared from Leghorn for Messina. He and the other Englishmen on board were discharged from the ship at Trieste on 6 Sept. 1789, with wages and prize money amounting to 230L. per man. During the interval the Saint Dinnan cruised in the Levant, took a large number of Turkish ships, robbed them of what was most valuable, murdered the crews, and burnt the vessels. The privateers also attacked and plundered some of the smaller Grecian islands. On one occasion they had a terrible combat with another pirate, who, after fighting all day, at length yielded. His ship had 378 men on board, 'all of different nations'. The survivors were told by their captors that they would be 'put to the cruelest death that ever could be invented. So we did, for next morning we got whips to the mainstay, and made one leg fast to the whip, and the other fast to a ringbolt in the deck, and so quartered them and hove them overboard.' These and other horrors Davidson narrates in plain methodical order.

The 'Bloody Journal', as it was called, came to have considerable renown with sailors, among whom it was probably current in manuscript versions. A copy was procured for Sir Walter Scott. ... Davidson probably found his position on the Niger exceedingly uncomfortable. He deserted from her at Portsmouth in November 1794, was afterwards pressed on board H.M.S. Royal George, and was accidentally drowned about 1795.

These were the savage and stoic 'articles' which were employed by Marlborough, Cumberland, Frederick, Germaine, Gates, Rodney, Nelson, Wellington, and the rest of them. They were articles which had sprung from a common compost-heap, the eighteenth-century Mob.

The political system of the Age of Scandal, a historian has beautifully written, was that of 'aristocracy tempered by rioting'. So aristocratic was it, that 'Pitt was

at first the only commoner in the Cabinet of 1783'
(Lecky), while Wilberforce refused a peerage because it
would exclude his children from intimacy with 'private
gentlemen of moderate fortunes, and clergymen, and,
still more, mercantile men'.

Admiral Palliser might use the article, but, if the
article's mother, the Mob, were displeased by the
admiral, his windows would be smashed and himself
burnt in effigy. Wellington might point at it in Brussels,
like a farmer at a pig, but, when the mother-mob found
him tardy about the Reform Bill, attempts would be
made in Fenchurch Street to drag him from his horse.
There was a give-and-take between the highest and the
lowest, a personal relationship, and, as the cabinet was
said to be the link between parliament and the administration, so the Mob mediated between the victor
of the Glorious First of June and the able seamen who
had fought there. Also, although the rewards of
admirals and generals were out of all proportion
superior to those of common men, these great people
did at least share and share alike with their followers in
the 'whirling of the bols', both at sea and on land.

The licence demanded by the Mob, and the good-
humour with which that licence was conceded in England, were surprising. In France, the lidded pot might
eventually boil over and scald the land with blood, but,
on the other side of the Channel, there was an openness
between the classes which allowed the vessel to let off
steam. Throughout the letters of Horace Walpole there
was an undercurrent of rioting, which was borne by the
sufferers without the least panic: riots about weaving,
in which the indignant Duke of Bedford received a
stone weighing six pounds; riots about Wilkes, in which
the Austrian Ambassador was taken out of his coach
by the trouserless, turned upside down, and the number

'45' chalked on the soles of his shoes; riots about an address to the King, in which a hearse was driven into St James's Palace, with an executioner and an axe on top, and during which the pugilistic Lord Talbot managed to bag a rioter; riots about printing libels, in which George Selwyn and Charles James Fox were rolled in the gutter, and King George was pelted with an apple; riots about tea, with the American mob dressed as Red Indians; riots about admirals, in which Pitt, Fox, and the Duke of Ancaster, drunk, joined the demonstrators and chose the best windows to smash; riots about Popery, in which it was rumoured that the lions had been loosed from the Tower menagerie; and riots about Peace, in which, according to Lord Onslow,

the insulting abuse offered to His Majesty was what I can never think of but with horror, nor ever forget what I felt when they proceeded to throw stones into the coach, several of which hit the King, which he bore with signal patience, but not without sensible marks of indignation and resentment at the indignities offered to his person and office. The glasses were all broken to pieces, and in this situation we were during our passage through the Park. The King took one of the stones out of the cuff of his coat, where it had lodged, and gave it to me, saying – 'I make you a present of this, as a mark of the civilities we have met with on our journey today.'

It was this indignation – this comic fuming at the 'disgraceful' behaviour of thousands who could easily have torn them limb from limb – this refusal to believe in the destructive capacity or in the seriously ill intentions of such amiable helots as surrounded them, which saved the English aristocracy from the guillotine. They refused to have the sense to realize that they were in danger, and the Mob, for lack of being taken seriously, remained comic.

The interesting feature of the disturbances was that life was seldom lost in them. For the crowd was an English one, with a cockney sense of humour, and the voice in the back row was available, which turned the dangerous situation to a laugh. In France they might massacre an ambassador, but they would hardly have turned him upside down to write on his boots. In England they might towzle the powdered wigs of half the House of Lords, but in France they would have cut their heads off. The sailors, weavers, harlots, chairmen, porters, and Protestants of the English metropolis adopted their riots as public holidays. The chairmen particularly seem to have had a sense of humour. Two of them, very drunk, carrying home the prim, terrified, and abstemious Mrs Herbert, opened the top of the chair and told her indistinctly: 'Madam, you are so drunk, that if you do not sit still, it will be impossible to carry you.'

Serious bloodshed took place only on one occasion, that of the Gordon Riots. Lord George Gordon was a maniac, who ended his life as an orthodox Jew, and he took occasion to foment the excitement arising from an attempt to alleviate the lot of Catholics, at that time labouring under civil disadvantages. The Mob was willing to pose as Protestant. On 2 June 1780, they assembled at Southwark to present an address against Popery. They marched to Westminster and commenced proceedings in the usual way. At the House of Lords, the Lords Townshend and Hillsborough had their wigs removed, and were left to enter with their back-hair round their ears; Lord Willoughby's periwig was violated; the Lord President of the Council had his shins hacked; the Archbishop of York had his sleeves torn off; and the fainting Bishop of Lincoln was scarcely rescued, from a neighbouring house, in female attire.

As bishop after bishop [said Jesse] entered the House of Lords with his lawn sleeves torn, and peer after peer with his hair hanging loose and his clothes covered with hair-powder, the scene grew more and more indecorous. 'It is hardly possible,' we are told, 'to conceive a more grotesque appearance than the House exhibited. Some of their Lordships with their hair about their shoulders; others smutted with dirt; most of them as pale as the ghost in Hamlet, and all of them standing up in their several places, and speaking at the same instant. One Lord proposing to send for the Guards; another for the Justices or Civil Magistrates; many crying out "Adjourn! Adjourn!" while the skies resounded with the huzzas, shoutings or hootings and hissings, in Palace Yard.'

The scene in the House of Commons was as remarkable; where, with the Mob surging outside, two gentlemen attended the raving Lord George Gordon, to plunge their swords into his heart, if he were to excite the tumult too far.

Next day, the pickpockets, burglars, and other disorderly persons began to take charge of the crowd. Looting and burning commenced. By the 6th the situation had passed out of hand, mansions were being stormed, fire employed, and jails were being delivered.

They broke the roof [wrote Crabbe], tore away the rafters, and, having got ladders, they descended. Not Orpheus himself had more courage, or better luck. Flames all around them, and a body of soldiers expected, they defied and laughed at all opposition. The prisoners escaped. I stood and saw about twelve women and eight men ascend from their confinement to the open air, and they were conducted through the streets in chains. Three of these were to be hanged on Friday. You have no conception of the frenzy of the multitude. This being done, and Akerman's house now a mere shell of brickwork, they kept a store of flame there for other purposes. It became red-hot, and the doors and windows appeared like the entrances to so many volcanoes. With some difficulty they then fired the debtors' prison, and they too all made their escape.

Lord Mansfield's house was burned to the ground, with its priceless library, and so were those of Sir John Fielding and many others. 'No Popery' was chalked, in self-defence, on all doors; except on the door of one humorist, who wrote 'No Religion'. On the 7th there were rumours that the lions from the Tower and the lunatics from Bedlam had been let loose. Horry Walpole came up from Strawberry to see the fun, and found Lord Hertford and his sons loading muskets. The Bank was attacked, the distillery of a rich Roman Catholic was stormed, giving drink to the rioters, and the Fleet, Marshalsea, and King's Bench prisons were broken open. The liberation of one miserable hold in Paris, the Bastille, had been anticipated by nine years.

The district most rife with low sensuality appears to have been the neighbourhood of Holborn Hill, where the conflagration raged the fiercest. The flames, bursting forth in volumes from the houses in Fleet Market, from the Fleet Prison, from Barnard's Inn, and from Langdale's Distillery, were rendered more terribly vivid in consequence of their being fed by the streams of burning spirits which flowed from the last-named establishment. In the fierce glare, men, women and children were to be seen rushing from their homes, carrying off such articles as they were most anxious to preserve. Pails full of gin were handed about among the crowd. Not only men, but women and children, were to be seen sucking up gin and other spirituous liquors, as they flowed along the kennels. Here and there lay drunken wretches on the ground in a state of insensibility. Some of the rioters, while in this state, are said to have perished in the flames; others to have literally drunk themselves to death.   JESSE

Wraxall could tell the time by the clock of St Andrew's Church, Holborn, in the light of the fires.

On 8 June, the King, by his own efforts, managed to pull the kingdom together, and troops were thrown into the fray. Horace Walpole saw a company of Horse Guards making for home, their bayonets steeped in blood. The Mob was cowed, their Protestant ribbons wrenched from their hats. Two hundred and eighty-five persons were killed by the military. Twenty-nine of those arrested remained to be hanged.

On the last day, an extraordinary change of heart took place. *Omne animal*, the aristocracy might have quoted – with the rest of the old saw. The wounded withdrew themselves in secrecy, without a word. The dead who had not been found by pickets were sur-reptitiously lowered into the black waters of the Fleet Ditch. No investigation was asked or offered, by Mob or Parliament. The scarlet road to Blackfriars Bridge was covered with fresh earth, as if by common consent; the bullet-scarred houses were re-plastered, nobody knew by whom, and, when London awoke on 9 June 1780, the blood-splashed walls of the Bank of England had been white-washed from top to bottom.

CHAPTER EIGHT

The Necrophilist

ONE evening when he was in high fettle, Horace Walpole sat down to make a catalogue of the latest *bons mots*. He recorded a joke of Chesterfield's and two cruel ones by Peter Le Neve and Old Craggs, the latter being about a person called Arthur Moore. Then he went on:

I told this story the other day to George Selwyn, whose passion is to see coffins and corpses, and executions: he replied, 'that Arthur Moore had had his coffin chained to that of his mistress'. – 'Lord!' said I, 'how do you know?' – 'Why, I saw them the other day in a vault at St Giles's.' He was walking this week in Westminster Abbey with Lord Abergavenny, and met the man who shews the tombs, 'Oh! your servant, Mr Selwyn; I expected to have seen you here the other day, when the old Duke of Richmond's body was taken up.' Shall I tell you another story of George Selwyn before I tap the chapter of Richmond, which you see opens here very *apropos*? With this strange and dismal turn, he has infinite fun and humour in him. He went lately on a party of pleasures to see places with Lord Abergavenny and a pretty Mrs Frere, who love one another a little. At Cornbury there are portraits of all the royalists and regicides, and illustrious headless. Mrs Frere ran about, looked at nothing, let him look at nothing, screamed about Indian paper, and hurried over all the rest. George grew peevish, called her back, told her it was monstrous, when he had come so far with her, to let him see nothing; 'And you are a fool, you don't know what you missed in the other room.' – 'Why what?' – 'Why, my Lord Holland's picture.' – 'Well! what

is my Lord Holland to me?' – 'Why, dont you know,' said
he, 'that my Lord Holland's body lies in the same vault in
Kensington church with my Lord Abergavenny's mother?'
Lord! she was so obliged, and thanked him a thousand
times.

The great letter-writers at the peak of the Age of
Scandal were thought to be Walpole and Selwyn – but
for a hundred years after their death there existed a
curious contrast between them. Horace had preserved
his own letters. He had even asked to have them back,
edited them, and caused fair copies to be made: a fact
which militates against their spontaneity. Selwyn had
preserved only the letters which were written to him by
others, and had, indeed, left strict instructions that his
own were to be destroyed. Horace was a circle which
existed by its centre, and Selwyn was defined by his
tangents. On a first inspection, this seemed humble and
charming on Selwyn's part, and arrogant on Walpole's.
Besides, it was not impossible to deduce Selwyn's character from the character of the letters which he received. It was like a parlour game. It may have seemed
to people of allusive mind in the nineteenth century
that his was the more subtle way of bidding for immortality.

George was born in 1719, the second son in a family
of Gloucestershire landowners who returned two members to Parliament for a rotten borough, and who consequently could count on their fair share of sinecures.
He was educated at Eton and at Oxford, and was sent
down from the latter with full anathema, because he
had celebrated the holy communion in a real chalice,
pretending to be Jesus Christ.

Acta Convocat. Univ. Oxon. Arch. 1745. (29th July) Die
lunae viz vicesimo nono mensis julii Ao Dom: 1745 causa
convocationis erat ut Georgius Augustus Selwyn nuper e

collegio Hertfordiensi Superioris ordinis commensalis gravissimi criminis insimulatus, quatenus institutionem coenae domini nostri Jesu Christi contumelioso et impio tractaverit tam nefani facinoris Hanc Domum ultricem sentiret –

Imprimis lecta erat Accusatio Tenoris subsequentis – The crimes wherewith George Augustus Selwyn, late of Hertford College, Gentleman Commoner, standeth charged, are these (viz.).

1. That on the twenty-first day of May last past, being drinking at a club, in company with several young noblemen and gentlemen of this University, at the house of one Charles Deverelle, an unlicensed seller of wines, near St Martin's Church in the City of Oxford, he the said George Augustus Selwyn did impiously affect to personate our Blessed Saviour, in His institution of the Holy Sacrament; and did ludicrously and profanely apply the words used by our Saviour at the said Institution, to the intemperate purposes of the said club.

2. That he the said George Augustus Selwyn did then and there take an old cup or chalice, which he had with no small pains provided for this wicked end, and did pour red wine into the same, and did cause the said Charles Deverelle to drink of the said wine in the said cup or chalice; and upon this, the said Selwyn's delivery of the said cup or chalice into the hands of him the said Deverelle, he the said Selwyn made use of these words, 'Drink this in remembrance of me –' or words to that effect.

3. That the said George Augustus Selwyn did afterwards then and there take the said cup or chalice, and having made signs as though he was blooding at one of his arms, did apply the neck of a bottle of wine into the said arm, from whence the said wine did gently distil into the said cup or chalice; whereupon the said Selwyn was heard to say, 'It bloods freely,' and that upon the refusal of one of the company to drink out of the said cup or chalice, he the said Selwyn did address himself unto that Person so refusing and upon this occasion did

make use of these words, 'Here's my body, Hoc est corpus meum – you know what it is in Greek – ' or to that effect.

On the death of the said George Augustus Selwyn's elder brother, the young man was left heir to the family property, and, at his father's death, became proprietor of the customary sinecures. He remained a man-about-town all his life, was a famous wit and gambler, and died in 1791 without having accomplished anything further than his scrape at Oxford. He never married. The reputation which he left behind, apart from that of wit, was that he was fond of going to executions, and partial to little girls.

The letters of Selwyn's friends threw a puzzling light upon his character; for, although all seemed to agree that he was a charming person, the letters themselves had a slight smell of rottenness. His clergyman toady, the Rev. Dr Warner, was a creature whom no decent being would have countenanced, yet his epistles were familiar and preserved with care, and the *tracasseries* about the child called Mie-Mie were unpleasant. Madame du Deffand, who was sentimental, said that George had no heart, and Horace Walpole observed in an unguarded moment that he was a *bête inspirée*. On the other hand, Selwyn long preserved the warm friendship of the Duke of Queensberry, who was honest in his wickedness, and who never would tolerate shams – not even from the Thames.

I remember dining [wrote William Wilberforce], when I was a young man, with the Duke of Queensberry, at his Richmond villa. The party was very small and select; Pitt, Lord and Lady Chatham, the Duchess of Gordon, and George Selwyn (who lived for society, and continued in it till he looked really like the wax-work figure of a corpse) were among the guests. We dined early, that some of our party might be ready to attend the Opera. The dinner was sumptuous, the views from the villa quite enchanting, and the Thames in all its glory; but the Duke looked on with indifference. 'What is there,' he said, 'to make so much of in the Thames? – I am quite tired of it, – there it goes, flow, flow, flow, always the same.'

Selwyn was loved by Horace Walpole himself, who wrote of him at his death:

I have had another and grievous memento, the death of poor Selwyn! His end was lovely, most composed and rational. From eight years old I had known him intimately without a cloud between us; few knew him so well, and consequently few knew so well the goodness of his heart and nature.

A better testimonial was the love of Lord Carlisle, a charming youth, but weak and impressionable and younger than the wit. It was better, because Carlisle had a better eye for friends than Walpole. Selwyn's acquaintances often assured him that they loved him, either because they did so, or else because they feared his tongue. Lord Holland used jokingly to assume, to his face, that he was a eunuch.

There were a dozen stories about Selwyn's interest in death, torture, and execution. He was supposed to frequent exhumations, and to have visited France in order to witness the horrid sufferings of Fr Damien, who was nipped with red-hot pincers and torn limb from limb by cart-horses, for having attempted the life of Louis XV. On that occasion he was said to have been accommodated with a grandstand view by one of the numerous executioners, who had asked, '*Êtes-vous bourreau?*' and who had been told by Selwyn, '*Non, Monsieur, je n'ai pas cet honneur; je ne suis qu'un amateur.*' It was at the same execution, incidentally, that a tender-hearted lady who was interested in the

prevention of cruelty to animals was said to have objected to the whipping of the horses, as inhuman, when they
were pulling Fr Damien to bits. The story about Selwyn
was apocryphal, and had also been told of La Condamine. Indeed, there was a regular incrustation of
legend to this particular martyrdom, for La Condamine,
who was deaf, was believed to have asked one of the
executioners what Damien was saying. '*Monsieur, il
jure horriblement.*' '*Ma foi, il a bien raison!*'

In the same way, many of the Selwyn stories sounded
too good to be true. 'You know', said Walpole, 'George
never thinks but *à la tête tranchée*: he came to town
t'other day to have a tooth drawn, and told the man
that he would drop his handkerchief for the signal.'
Lord Holland, on his death bed, told the servant: 'The
next time Mr Selwyn calls, show him up: if I am alive,
I shall be delighted to see him, and if I am dead he will
be glad to see me.' Gilly Williams, George Townshend,
Lord Carlisle, even the King, made jokes about his pen-
chant. Wraxall was assured that he went to executions
in female attire.

Apart from the jokes, which he seldom resented,
there was a substratum of morbidity. Walpole related
an unpleasant story of his activities. 'A footman of
Lord Dacre has been hanged for murdering the butler.
George Selwyn had a great hand in bringing him to
confess it. That Selwyn should be a capital performer
in a scene of that kind is not extraordinary: I tell it you
for the strange coolness which the young fellow, who
was but nineteen, expressed: as he was writing his confession, "I murd –" he stopped, and asked, "How do
you spell *murdered*?"'

Selwyn received letters such as the following: 'Har-
rington's porter was condemned yesterday. Cadogan
and I have already bespoken places at the Brazier's, and

I hope Parson Digby will come time enough to be of the party. I presume we shall have your honour's company, if your stomach is not too squeamish for a single swing.' When he was not at a hanging, his friends took care to send him a description.

The best tale of his Ingoldsby-legendary leanings was told by Horace Walpole, in his description of the execution of Lord Lovat – a description which it is impossible not to quote in full.

Arlington Street, March 20, 1747

I have been living at old Lovat's trial, and was willing to have it over before I talked to you of it. It lasted seven days: the evidence was as strong as possible; and after all he had denounced, he made no defence ... The old creature's behaviour has been foolish, and at last indecent. I see little parts in him, nor attribute much to that cunning for which he is so famous: it might catch wild Highlanders; but the art of dissimulation and flattery is so refined and improved, that it is of little use now where it is not very delicate. His character seems a mixture of tyranny and pride in his villainy. I must make you a little acquainted with him. In his own domain he governed despotically, either burning or plundering the lands and houses of his open enemies, or taking off his secret ones by the assistance of his cook, who was his poisoner in chief. He had two servants who married without his consent; he said, 'You shall have enough of each other,' and stowed them in a dungeon, that had been a well, for three weeks. When he came to the Tower, he told them, that if he were not so old and infirm, they would find it difficult to keep him there. They told him they had kept much younger: 'Yes,' said he, 'but they were inexperienced: they had not broke so many gaols as I have.' At his own house he used to say, that for thirty years of his life he never saw a gallows but it made his neck ache. His last act was to shift his treason upon his eldest son, whom he forced into the rebellion. He told Williamson, the Lieutenant of the Tower, 'We will hang my eldest son, and then my second shall marry your niece.' He has a sort of ready humour at repartee, not very well adapted to his situation. One day that Williamson complained that he could not sleep, he was so haunted with *rats* – he replied, 'What do you say, that you are so haunted with *Ratcliffes*?' The first day, as he was brought to his trial, a woman looked into the coach, and said, 'You ugly old dog, don't you think you will have that frightful head cut off?' He replied, 'You ugly old – , I believe I shall.' At his trial he affected great weakness and infirmities, but often broke out into passions; particularly at the first witness, who was his vassal: he asked him how he dared to come thither! ... The two last days he behaved ridiculously, joking, and making everybody laugh even at his sentence. He said to Lord Ilchester, who sat near the bar, 'Je meurs pour ma patrie, et ne m'en soucie gueres.' When he withdrew, he said, 'Adieu! my lords, we shall never meet again in the same place.' He says he will be hanged; for that his neck is so short and bended, that he should be struck in the shoulders. I did not think it possible to feel so little as I did at so melancholy a spectacle, but tyranny and villainy wound up by buffoonery took off all edge of concern.

Arlington Street, April 10, 1747

I deferred writing to you as long as they deferred the execution of old Lovat, because I had a mind to send you some account of his death, as I had of his trial. He was beheaded yesterday, and died extremely well, without passion, affectation, buffoonery, or timidity; his behaviour was natural and intrepid. He professed himself a Jansenist; made no speech, but sat down a little while in a chair on the scaffold, and talked to the people round him. He said, 'He was glad to suffer for his country, *dulce est pro patria mori*; that he did not know how, but he had always loved it, *nescio qua natale solum &c.*; that he had never swerved from his principles; that this was the character of his family, who had been gentlemen for five hundred years.' He lay down quietly, gave the sign soon, and was despatched at a blow. I believe it will strike some terror into the Highlands, when

Westminster School

Taste in high life

c. Sir Robert Walpole

b. Horace Walpole

a. John, Lord Hervey (Sporus)

Gin Lane

George Selwyn and his dog Râton

Miss Chudleigh in the character of Iphigenia at the
Venetian Ambassador's masquerade

Admiral Byng

Credulity, superstition, and fanaticism

Dr Johnson

Carolina Matilda

Le Marquis de Sade

Fast Day

they hear there is any power great enough to bring so potent a tyrant to the block. A scaffold fell down and killed several persons; one, a man that had rid post from Salisbury the day before to see the ceremony; and a woman was taken up dead with a live child in her arms.

Arlington Street, April 16, 1747

You have heard that old Lovat's tragedy is over: it has been succeeded by a little farce, containing the humours of the Duke of Newcastle. ... The first event was a squabble between his Grace and the Sheriff about holding up the head on the scaffold – a custom that has been disused, and which the Sheriff would not comply with, as he received no order in writing. Since that, the Duke has burst ten yards of breeches strings about the body, which was to be sent into Scotland; but it seems it is customary for vast numbers to rise to attend the most trivial burial. The Duke, who is always at least as much frightened at doing right as at doing wrong, was three days before he got courage enough to order the burying in the Tower. I must tell you an excessive good story of George Selwyn: Some women were scolding him for going to see the execution, and asked him, how he could be such a barbarian as to see the head cut off? 'Nay,' says he, 'if that was such a crime, I am sure I have made amends, for I went to see it sewed on again.' When he was at the undertakers, as soon as they had stitched him together, and were going to put the body into the coffin, George, in my Lord Chancellor's voice, said 'My Lord Lovat, your lordship may rise.'

Selwyn took an interest in more than one small girl, but his complicated relationship with the one called Mie-Mie was the passion of his life. She was the natural daughter of his friend the Duke of Queensberry, by an Italian Marchioness, and it was long thought that Selwyn disputed her paternity in the belief that he was himself the father. It is clear from the letters that this was not the case. So far as his attitude was defined, he appeared to have taken a fancy to the child as a baby, pitied it, disapproved of its parents, and taken it under his wing. He ended by fighting a protracted battle with the mother, who wanted to keep it, while Queensberry looked on with amused contempt; and he chased Mie-Mie up and down Europe until he finally secured her person. His letters to harassed headmistresses about her health and spirits were only less funny than the answers from the headmistresses. 'Mrs Terry presents her best compliments to Mr Selwyn: is very sorry to find he is so uneasy. The dear child's spirits are *not* depressed. She is very lively: ate a good dinner: and behaves just like any other children.' He spent the rest of his life doting upon her, and left her £33,000, in addition to the £150,000 which was left to her by Old Q. Understandably enough, she grew up to marry the wicked Lord Yarmouth, was separated from him, travelled on the Continent with a lover, was believed to be the mother of Sir Richard Wallace, and figured in *Vanity Fair* as the Marchioness of Steyne.

The third main trait deducible from contemporary evidence was Selwyn's wit.

Humour is an article which seems to have two compartments, permanent and temporary, the latter being the larger. It is subject to fashion. 'Real mirth', wrote Dr Johnson in his *Lives of the Poets*, 'must always be natural, and nature is uniform. Men have been wise in very different modes, but they have always laughed the same way.' Mrs (Thrale) Piozzi, who was no fool, wrote in the margin: 'I think *not*; I think national mirth a great discrimination of national character. Wisdom is dressed up alike by almost all. . . . One way of being wise, I think, and a thousand of being merry. . . .' There seem to be some kinds of humour which remain amusing through the centuries and across geography, and perhaps there are some kinds of wit also – usually the wit of abstract ideas rather than of personalities – which may be superior to time and space. Possibly Chinamen, possibly people of the thirtieth century, may smile at Falstaff or at the fun of Sydney Smith, with its affectionate glee. Somebody once asked the latter if a bishop were going to marry. 'Perhaps he may. Yet how can a bishop marry? How can he flirt? The most he can say is, "I will see you in the vestry after service."' Finding a boy stroking a tortoise, he asked, 'Why are you doing that?' 'Oh, to please the tortoise.' 'Why, child, you might as well stroke the dome of St Paul's, to please the Dean and Chapter.' When a beautiful young lady cried out in the garden, 'Oh, Mr Sydney, you will never bring this pea to perfection', he took her gravely by the hand and, leading her forward, said: 'Then allow me to bring perfection to the pea.'

In opposition to this happy fun, there is the wit of personalities and of fashion, which is as impermanent as the fashions themselves. The harsh Jest Books of court Fools under Henry VIII or James I are as dry as blue-books to us. Archie Hamilton cannot raise a grin. Perhaps it was because the wit of fashion was unkind and destructive, where Sydney Smith's was loving, that 'wit' as such did not retain its pleasantry.

It was to the second form of humour that the main body of Selwyn's wit belonged. His jokes are lamentable now, however successful then. They were in the punning mode, and used as 'hits'.

A luckless traveller called Bruce, whose truthful stories about Abyssinia were doomed to be disbelieved because nobody else had been there, had been saying that among their musical instruments the Ethiopians played upon a kind of lyre. Selwyn whispered, like any schoolboy, that there was one liar less since Bruce had left the country. When a Mr Foley had fled to France because of his debts, Selwyn commented that it was a pass-over which would not be relished by the Jews. When a man called Fox had been hanged, and Charles James Fox asked him if he had been to the execution, he observed: 'No, Charles, I make a point of never attending rehearsals.' It was heartless stuff – but sometimes he rose to higher levels. Walpole, remarking on the similar governments of George II and George III, mentioned that there was nothing new under the sun. 'Nor,' said Selwyn, 'under the grandson.' Asked if Princess Amelia would have a guard, he replied with some indelicacy, 'Now and then one, I suppose.'

Wraxall explained Selwyn's jokes by saying that 'the effect when falling from his lips became greatly augmented by the listless and drowsy manner in which he uttered them, for he always seemed half asleep'. This was the clue to the enigma. He possessed the play-actor's flair which made a stupid remark seem funny for the time being: the 'business' which actors exhibit by raising their eyebrows, like George Robey, or by looking pained and grieved. Selwyn's drooping eyelids and demure look, which Reynolds drew with care, helped him to look sleepy.

This, in turn, for those who share Dr Johnson's contempt for the essential emptiness of actors, leads to the real Selwyn: to the centre which had been wise enough to exist by its tangents, and to direct the destruction of its letters. By some oversight, his own letters were not destroyed after all. They began to be published in 1897, by the Historical Manuscripts Commission, and the mystery of his character was cleared at once.

To put it bluntly, it turned out that the great wit of Almack's had been a shallow, complaining, and ignorant valetudinarian. He had written in a mixture of poor

English, bad French, and worse Italian. After all the talk of the 'monstrous good things' which George had said, the letters which came to light were the ill-spelt and endless chatter of an empty-headed fellow – a laughing stock even, who had suffered the indignity, not only of falling in love with a baby that called him Yan-Yan, but also of catching the whooping cough from it at the age of sixty-one.

Mimi never went out to air in the coach, never ate, or did anything, without Selwyn attending her. When she began to grow up, she used to treat him with offensive disrespect. She took the tone, which many of the young men of the time had done, of treating him, this great wit, this father of all the *bons mots* that were circulating in London, as tiresome, and what is called a bore. ... However, Mlle Fagniani's treatment of him did not in any degree diminish his sort of maternal fondness and partiality towards her. Looking at her one day, he said to Storer, 'What a pleasure it is to love that girl so tenderly without having had the trouble to get her' ... Storer says that Selwyn professed never to have had connexion with a woman but seven times in the whole course of his life, and that the last time was with a maid at the Inn at Andover, when he was 29. Yet he was a stout, healthy man, and never had any less natural taste or appetite imputed to him. But he undoubtedly had a fondness for the Duke of Queensberry ... and Lord Carlisle, which had all the extravagance and blindness of passion. His attachment to them has been called a sort of sentimental sodomy. ... He had also latterly, as I have heard, fallen into the error of almost all men who love wit and anecdote, when they become old, that of telling too many stories, and the same story too often. The Duke of Queensberry used to treat him always as much his inferior in understanding.

GLENBERVIE

CHAPTER NINE

Romance

So melodramatic was the latter part of the eighteenth century, so much the reverse of an Age of Reason in which the *via media* could be followed, that the strain of living in those decades might have intimidated a cowboy. The heaths sprinkled with highwaymen and gibbets, the towns patrolled by window-smashing mobs, the people of the sea-ports ready to fly from the pressgangs or from the smugglers, London rich in brothels which were called *bagnios* and in gin shops where it was possible to 'get drunk for a penny or dead drunk for twopence', the housewives of Edinburgh hurling out their slops from upper windows with the cry of 'Gardyloo' (*gardez l'eau*) while the foot passengers screamed out 'Haud yer han' and ran for their lives, macaronis in the midnight lanes fighting battles with the watchmen, and gentlemen still wearing swords on formal occasions, which were for use as well as for ornament: with these *agrémens*, the life of the aristocracy was not a sinecure.

William IV [says Lecky] was accustomed to relate how his great-grandfather George II, when walking alone in Kensington Gardens, was robbed by a single highwayman who climbed over the wall, and pleading his great distress, and with a manner of much deference, deprived the King of his purse, his watch, and his buckles. Even in the most central parts of London, highway robberies were not infrequent. Thus, George IV, when Prince of Wales, and the Duke of York were robbed on Hay Hill near Berkeley

Square. Two daughters of Admiral Holborn were driving across St James's Square on their return from the Opera, when a single footpad stopped their carriage and carried off their watches and jewels. The Neapolitan Ambassador, though two footmen stood behind his carriage, was stopped in Grosvenor Square and robbed of his watch and money. ... At Kensington, as late as the beginning of the present [19th] century, it was customary on Sunday evenings to ring a bell at intervals, in order that the pleasure seekers from London might assemble in sufficient numbers to return in safety.

Even an old maid like Horace Walpole was prepared to catch a housebreaker for the morbid Selwyn to hang, with the same indulgence as one might collect a caterpillar for a favourite nephew.

Last Sunday night, being as wet a night as you shall see in a summer's day, about half an hour after twelve, I was just come home from White's, and undressing to step into bed, I heard Harry, who you know lies forwards, roar out, 'Stop thief!' and run down stairs. I ran after him. Don't be frightened; I have not lost one enamel, nor bronze, nor have been shot through the head again. [He had been missed by a highwayman on a previous occasion.] A gentlewoman who lives at Governor Pitt's, next door but one to me ... called out 'watch'; two men, who were sentinels, ran away, and Harry's voice after them. Down came I, and with a posse of chairmen and watchmen found the third fellow in the area of Mr Freeman's house. Mayhap you have seen all this in the papers, little thinking who commanded the detachment. Harry fetched a blunderbuss to invite the thief up. One of the chairmen, who was drunk, cried, 'Give me the blunderbuss, I'll shoot him!' But as the general's head was a little cooler, he prevented military execution, and took the prisoner without bloodshed, intending to make his triumphal entry into the metropolis of Twickenham with his captive tied to the wheels of his post-chaise. I find my style rises so much with the recollection of my victory, that I don't know how to descend to tell you that the enemy was a carpenter, and had a leather apron on. The next step was to share my glory with my friends. I despatched a courier to White's for George Selwyn, who, you know, loves nothing upon earth so well as a criminal, except the execution of him. It happened very luckily that the drawer, who received my message, had very lately been robbed himself, and had the wound fresh in his memory. He stalked up into the club-room, stopped short, and with a hollow trembling voice said, 'Mr Selwyn! Mr Walpole's compliments to you, and he has got a housebreaker for you!' A squadron immediately came to reinforce me, and having summoned Moreland with the keys of the fortress, we marched into the house to search for more of the gang. Col. Seabright with his sword drawn went first, and then I, exactly the figure of Robinson Crusoe, with a candle and lanthorn in my hand, a carbine upon my shoulder, my hair wet and about my ears, and in a linen night-gown and slippers. We found the kitchen shutters forced, but not finished; and in the area a tremendous bag of tools, a hammer large enough for the hand of a jael, and six chisels!

The life of alarms and excursions was lived by a society whose outlook, moreover, was ceasing to be classical. They knew too much about the classics to find them novel or exhilarating. On the contrary, it was the Gothic, the Eastern, the Celtic, anything not connected with ancient Rome, which had begun to intoxicate the period. The 'Druid' was a special invention of the Age of Scandal. An elderly gentleman in a nightshirt and mistletoe, who denounced the Plantagenet kings from some majestic crag in Snowdonia, the Druid bore little relationship to the cannibals and duk-duk dancers of Gaelic prehistory. It was the age of the grotto. 'Here, John,' the Rev. William Bowles (1762–1850) would say, when visitors called, 'run with the crucifix and the missal to the hermitage, and set the fountain going.'

The 'awfulness' of Swiss scenery was what made every-body shudder, and between 1750 and 1795 there were no less than sixty books published about travels in Switzerland. *Rasselas, Ossian, Caractacus, Vathek,* Percy's *Reliques,* or the *Castle of Otranto* were the latest rage, and people were so excited by the non-classical renaissance, at least thirty years before the birth of Keats, that they could scarcely wait to realize the Gothick dream. Indeed, they seldom did wait to realize it. It generally collapsed in ruin upon their infatuated heads, for lack of tiresome details like foundations. Walpole's vision of Strawberry Hill was erected in such a hurry that there was no time to supply it with real tracery: it had to be painted on paper, which peeled off. Beckford's night-mare abbey at Fonthill had a tower three hundred feet high, nearly high enough for a pupil to manoeuvre an aeroplane with safety, which fell down as soon as it had been put up. He put it up again, with feverish energy, but down it came once more. Even the Lords Mayor were touched with the medieval romance in their banquets, as late as 1819, and even their attempt to realize it fell down.

The company assembled in the hall [wrote Creevey] were nine hundred in number, ladies and gentlemen, at five tables. . . . We were marched entirely round the hall, till we arrived at the top, where a table on a slight elevation went across the hall for us guests. Western's great delight was three men in complete armour from top to toe, with im-mense plumes of feathers upon their helmets. They were seated in three niches in the wall over our table. . . . It was their duty to rise and wave their truncheons when the Lord Mayor rose and gave the toasts; which they did with great effect, till one of them fainted away with the heat and fell out of his hole upon the heads of the people below.

The slapstick of the age was balanced by a romantic

eccentricity in vice, by a macabre virility, which equalled that of the Restoration or of the Elizabethan dramatists. Webster and Tourneur had not imagined any horrors which were not attempted in the Age of Scandal. 'I am glad you are aware of Miss Pitt,' wrote Horace Walpole. 'Her very first slip was with her eldest brother; and it is not her fault that she has not made still blacker trips.' Incest was the *frisson* of the century, as homosexuality was to be that of the twentieth. Nearly everybody dealt with it, from Walpole to Byron. The Marquis de Sade, in real life not a very sensational person, would have paled beside Mrs Brownrigg, who whipped her apprentices to death. A Mr Waddy in the Irish troubles ate half a priest (Barrington, 1. 264). A lover of the wife of George I was murdered on leaving her bedroom and buried under the stairs. George II's brother-in-law was a maniac who tried to kill his son. George III's sister was nearly beheaded in Denmark, and her lover Struensee was beheaded. George IV caused his wife to be tried for adultery, an offence which might have been punishable by the axe, as high treason.

Some of the stories in Walpole are still almost too horrible for print:

Having no more public events to tell you, I am sorry I must leap to a private story, in which there is far from being either bravery or gallantry, but which is savage enough to have been transmitted from the barbarians on the Mosquito shore. ... Well! but my story comes only 'cross the Irish Channel. Lord C., a recent peer of that kingdom, and married to a great heiress there, a very amiable woman, had, however, a more favourite mistress. The nymph, like My Lord, was no mirror of constancy, but preferred a younger, handsomer swain. The Peer, frantic with jealousy, discovered an assignation, and, hiring four bravoes, broke in upon the lovers; when, presenting a pistol to the head of his rival, he bade him make instant option of being shot, or reduced to the inability of giving any man jealousy. The poor young man was so ungallant as to prefer a chance for life on any terms. The brutal Lord ordered his four ruffians to seize the criminal, and with his own hand performed the bloody operation. The victim died the next day, the murderer escaped, but one of his accomplices is taken.

If these people were to be considered as cold and classical, if the pathetic bourgeoisie of the succeeding century were to be regarded as 'romantic' in opposition to them, then the meaning of words must have lost reality.

As for their women, in contrast to the dowdy blue-stockings who consorted with the poets of the nineteenth century, the beauties who were the contemporaries of Walpole lived through romances of such intricacy and splendour that Hollywood in delirium would scarcely do them justice.

Quand la charette passe devant le Palais-Royal [said Saint-Amand of the execution of Madame Du Barry], la victime aperçoit le balcon d'une maison de modes où plusieurs ouvrières regardent le funèbre cortège. Cette maison, elle la reconnaît; c'est là où, toute jeune fille, elle travaillait comme apprentie modiste. Hélas! pourquoi est-elle devenue Madame la comtesse Du Barry? Ses traits sont alternativement d'une pâleur livide et d'une rouge foncé. Elle se débat au milieu de l'exécuteur et de ses deux aides, qui ont peine à la retenir sur le banc. Ses cris redoublent. 'La vie! la vie! dit-elle, qu'on me laisse la vie, et je donne tous mes biens à la nation.' Alors, dans la foule, un homme réplique: 'Tu ne donnes à la nation que ce qui lui appartient, puisque le tribunal vient de les confisquer, tes biens.' Un charbonnier, placé devant cet homme, se retourne, et lui donne un soufflet. La victime recommence ses supplications. 'Mes amis, s'écrie-t-elle, mes amis, je n'ai jamais fait de mal a personne! Au

nom du ciel, je vous en prie, sauvez-moi!' Qui sait? les
tricoteuses elles-mêmes, les furies qui lèchent la guillotine
vont peut-être s'émouvoir à ces accents de la femme du
peuple. Cette fois ce n'est pas une reine qui va mourir, c'est
une comtesse, mais une comtesse qui a d'abord été ouvrière.
On fouette les chevaux, on brusque le dénoûment pour
arrêter la compassion de la foule. Enfin la charette arrive
sur la place qui s'appelait autrefois place Louis XV; là, où
s'élevait naguère la statue du monarque, est dressé l'écha-
faud où l'on supplicie sa maîtresse. Il est quatre heures et
demie. 'A moi, s'écrie-t-elle; à moi! Grâce! grâce! monsieur le bourreau! Encore . . .' Le couperet tombe, Madame
Du Barry a vécu!

If the little seamstress's life had been tragic, it had at
least been uninhibited, as were the lives of many of her
sisters on both sides of the Channel. Some of these
ladies, like Lady Harriet Wentworth, eloped with their
footmen: some, like Mrs Murray, were attempted by
their footmen to be ravished. A prostitute called Nancy
Parsons, after living with the Dukes of Dorset and
Grafton, married Lord Maynard and was described in
the peerages as 'widow of — Horton Esq.' The illegiti-
mate daughter of a milliner did better than Madame
Du Barry, and became the sister-in-law of George III.

A Lady Cathcart who died in 1789 had married a
Captain Macguire for her fourth husband, but had
displeased him by wearing a ring on which was written:

> If I survive
> I will have five.

The editor [wrote Maria Edgeworth] was acquainted with
Colonel M'Guire, Lady Cathcart's husband; he has lately
seen and questioned the maid-servant who lived with
Colonel M'Guire during the time of Lady Cathcart's imprisonment. Her ladyship was locked up in her own house
for many years, during which period her husband was

visited by the neighbouring gentry, and it was his regular
custom at dinner to send his compliments to Lady Cathcart,
informing her that the company had the honour to drink
her ladyship's health, and begging to know whether there
was anything at table she would like to eat? The answer was
always, 'Lady Cathcart's compliments, and she has everything she wants.' . . . At Colonel M'Guire's death her ladyship was released. The editor, within this year, saw the
gentleman who accompanied her to England after her
husband's death. When she first was told of his death she
imagined that the news was not true, and that it was told
only with an intention of deceiving her. At his death she had
scarcely clothes sufficient to cover her; she wore a red wig,
looked scared, and her understanding seemed stupefied; she
said that she scarcely knew one human creature from
another; her imprisonment lasted above twenty years.

Why she called herself Cathcart when she was married to M'Guire or Macguire is not explained, and unfortunately he does not figure in the *Dictionary of
National Biography*. But it seems that in the sequel she
did have her fifth husband. In any case, she danced at
the Welwyn Assembly, a free woman, when past eighty,
and lived to be ninety-eight.

In this respect she was more fortunate than the Lady
Grant mentioned by Boswell:

The true story of this lady, which happened in this century,
is as frightfully romantick as if it had been the fiction of a
gloomy fancy. She was the wife of one of the Lords of Session
in Scotland, a man of the very first blood of his country. For
some mysterious reasons, which have never been discovered, she was seized and carried off in the dark, she
knew not by whom, and by nightly journeys was conveyed
to the Highland shores, from whence she was transported by
sea to the remote rock of St Kilda, where she remained,
amongst its few wild inhabitants, a forlorn prisoner, but had
a constant supply of provisions, and woman to wait on her.

No inquiry was made after her, till she at last found means to convey a letter to a confidential friend, by the daughter of a catechist, who concealed it in a clue of yarn. Information being thus obtained at Edinburgh, a ship was sent to bring her off; but intelligence of this being received, she was conveyed to M'Leod's island of Herries, where she died.

All this was small romance, moreover, compared with the stories of the leading stars.

The notorious Miss Chudleigh began by fascinating the Earl of Bath and nearly married the Duke of Hamilton. She became a maid-of-honour, clandestinely wedded the future Earl of Bristol, had a son by him in secret, went to a ball in a gauze dress, and caught the eye of George II. He overcame his meanness to the extent of presenting her with a watch which cost him thirty-five guineas, 'out of his own privy purse and not charged on the civil list'. She also made a conquest of Frederick II, who admired her ability to swallow two bottles of wine. 'When reproached by her royal mistress,' said Wraxall, 'for the irregularities of her conduct, "*Votre Altesse Royale sait*," replied she, "*que chacun a son But.*"' (The Altesse Royale was believed to be the mistress of Lord Bute.) Fearing that the Earl of Bristol might die before the marriage could be acknowledged, and that she might lose her secret title, she had taken pains to have the marriage entered by underhand means in the church register. Now, however, she became the whore of the Duke of Kingston, and saw her chance to become a duchess. Complicated *tracasseries* ended in her marriage to the Duke, while the Earl was still alive. When the Duke died, he left her his immense fortune, and she went off to Italy, to vamp Pope Clement XIV. Unfortunately, the story of her bigamous marriage had got about, and it was in the interest of the Duke's other heirs to prove that she was really the Countess of

Bristol. It became necessary for her to tamper with the marriage register once again, this time in order to destroy it. The coil was too difficult. She was brought to trial before the House of Lords, found guilty, and barely escaped from being branded in the hand. The Countess-Duchess was now demoted to a countess, but for some reason she was left in possession of the fortune. The Earl of Bristol was unable to divorce her, because there was evidence of his collusion in the bigamy. She retired to Russia, where she got on well with her sister in frailty, Catherine the Great, and thence to France, where she purchased a royal palace for £50,000. She died at sixty-eight, in 1788, after other love affairs, and after receiving an offer of marriage from Prince Radzivil. Her picture as she appeared in the gauze dress still survives, wearing a ravishing smirk. It is a single garment, quite transparent, and probably explains her career. Throughout her life, she had enjoyed two or more of everything that was obtainable, counting the husbands and the bottles of wine. When a two-headed calf was born in Essex, Horace Walpole suggested that it must be hers. Sir Robert Keith said that he would be willing to marry her, if a grenadier might be joined with him in the nuptials. Other wags reported that she had given birth to twins, thus offering Lord Chesterfield the opportunity for one of his greatest *mots*. She mentioned the scandal to him with simulated indignation, on which his Lordship answered politely: 'Madam, I make a point of never believing more than half of what I hear.'

The high romance of the age was the career of the lovely Misses Gunning.

The two penniless Irish girls had been brought to England by their father, John Gunning of Castle Coote, when they were about eighteen years of age, in 1751.

Walpole considered that their beauty depended upon there being two of them, 'for singly I have seen much handsomer women than either'. Whatever the explanation, they 'made more noise than any of their predecessors since the days of Helen'. Their loveliness was so great that it was a nuisance to them. Once, when they went to Hampton Court, and were examining the Beauty Room there, the housekeeper brought another party, saying, 'This way, ladies, here are the Beauties.' The Gunnings, who had been persecuted by curious mobs already, supposed that this was a reference to their own charms, and flew into a passion, exclaiming that they had come 'to see the palace, not to be shown as a sight themselves'. The misunderstanding was not unnatural, for on one occasion seven hundred people sat up all night to see them leave an inn in Yorkshire, and, on another, a shoemaker in Worcester made two and a half guineas by exhibiting a shoe which he had made for one of them, at a penny a head. In later life, this one had to be protected by a guard of soldiers, when walking in Hyde Park.

The younger sister's marriage was the more brilliant, the elder's the more tragic. Both were dazzling.

The younger of them married the Duke of Hamilton with a ring of the bed-curtain at half past twelve at night, in Mayfair Chapel, and was presented at Court. 'The crowd was so great that even the noble crowd in the Drawing Room clambered upon chairs and tables to look at her.' She was carried to the north by her Duke, where, said Walpole, 'her history is not unentertaining; Duke Hamilton is the abstract of Scotch pride; he and his Duchess, at their own house, walk in to dinner before the company; sit together at the upper end of the table; eat off the same plate; and drink to nobody beneath the rank of Earl.' Hamilton died in

1758, and she then married the Duke of Argyll, taking with her a good portion of the Hamilton pride. She had a spirited brush with the resilient Boswell when he was trundling Dr Johnson round Scotland – owing to the fact that Boswell had opposed her in a law-suit. The description of the dinner-party at which she dealt with him was a piece of high comedy, but unfortunately too long to quote as an aside, except in fragments:

As I was going away, the duke said, 'Mr Boswell, won't you have some tea?' – I thought it best to get over the meeting with the duchess this night; so respectfully agreed. I was conducted to the drawing room by the duke, who announced my name; but the duchess, who was sitting with her daughter, Lady Betty Hamilton, and some other ladies, took not the least notice of me ... [Next day]: The Duke placed Dr Johnson next himself at table. I was in fine spirits; and though sensible that I had the misfortune of not being in favour with the duchess, I was not in the least disconcerted, and offered her grace some of the dish that was before me ... I knew it was the rule of modern high life not to drink to anybody; but that I might have the satisfaction for once to look the duchess in the face, with a glass in my hand, I with a respectful air addressed her, – 'My Lady Duchess, I have the honour to drink your grace's good health.'

Evidently poor Bozzy had not been told the story about the 'rank of Earl'. He got no reply to this either, but, after much more:

I made some remark that seemed to imply a belief in *second sight*. The duchess said, 'I fancy you will be a *Methodist*.' – This was the only sentence her grace deigned to utter to me; and I take it for granted, she thought it a good hit on my *credulity* in the Douglas cause. ...

We went to tea. The duke and I walked up and down the drawing-room, conversing. The duchess still continued to shew the same marked coldness for me; for which, though I suffered from it, I made every allowance, considering the very warm part I had taken for Douglas . . . .

Her grace made Dr Johnson come and sit by her, and asked him why he made his journey so late in the year. 'Why, madam (said he), you know Mr Boswell must attend the Court of Session, and it does not rise till the 12th of August.' – she said, with some sharpness, 'I *know nothing* of Mr Boswell.' . . . I indeed felt it rather too severe, but when I recollected that my punishment was inflicted by so dignified a beauty, I had that kind of consolation which a man would feel who is strangled by a *silken cord*.

It was this double-duchess who sat in the coach with Queen Charlotte, when she was being brought to London to marry George III, and who smiled at her fears of matrimony. 'You may laugh,' said the Queen. 'You have been married twice. But to me it is no joke.'

'Considering,' said Jesse, 'that personal beauty was the sole dowry of the Duchess of Hamilton and Argyll, it is remarkable that the untitled daughter of an Irish gentleman should have been the wife of two dukes and the mother of four.' He might have added that she also refused the hand of a third duke, his Grace of Bridgewater.

The elder daughter's match was with Lord Coventry. Her simple and pathetic story comes through the pages of Walpole clearly; for she was silly, loving, honest, and without pretence.

I cant say her genius is equal to her beauty; she every day says some new *sproposito*. She has taken a turn of vast fondness for her new lord: Lord Downe met them at Calais, and offered her a tent-bed, for fear of the bugs in the inns, 'Oh!' said she, 'I had rather be bit to death than lie one night from my dear Cov.!'

If Lady Coventry anticipated [wrote Jesse], in the gay circles of Paris, the same triumph which her beauty had obtained for her in the fashionable society of London, she was destined to be signally disappointed. Our beauties [writes Walpole] are returned. The French would not conceive ... that my Lady Coventry has much pretence to be so [handsome] now. Indeed all the travelled English allow that there is a Madame de Brionne handsomer, and a finer figure. Poor Lady Coventry was under piteous disadvantages; for besides being very silly, ignorant of the world, breeding, speaking no French, and suffered to wear neither red nor powder, she had that perpetual drawback upon her beauty, her lord, who is sillier in a wise way, as ignorant, ill-bred, and speaking very little French himself — just enough to shew how ill-bred he is. The Duke de Luxemburg told him he had called up my Lady Coventry's coach; my lord replied, *Vous avez fort bien fait*. He is jealous, prude, and scrupulous. At a dinner at Sir John Bland's, before sixteen persons, he coursed his wife round the table, on suspecting she had stolen on a little red, seized her, scrubbed it off by force with a napkin, and then told her that since she had deceived him and broke her promise, he would carry her back directly to England. They were pressed to stay for the great *fête* at St Cloud; he excused himself, because it would make him miss a music meeting at Worcester! and she excused herself from the fireworks at Madame Pompadour's, because it was her dancing-master's hour! I will tell you but one more anecdote, and I think you cannot be imperfect in your ideas of them. The Maréchale de Lowendahl was pleased with an English fan Lady Coventry had, who very civilly gave it her; my lord made her write for it again next morning, 'because he had given it her before marriage, and her parting with it would make an irreparable breach,' and send an old one in the room of it! She complains to every body she meets, how odd it is that my lord should use her so ill, when she knows that he has so great a regard that he would die for her, and when he was so good as to marry her without a shilling!

That Lady Coventry ... wanted tact and discernment ... there is every reason to believe. George the Second, at the close of his long life, was ... regretting, for her sake, that there had been no masquerades during the year: 'As for sights,' said the inconsiderate beauty, 'she was quite satisfied with them; there was only one that she was eager to see, and that was a Coronation!' ...

If Lady Coventry, however, was a simpleton, she was at least a good natured one [Horace Walpole writes to George Montagu, 20 April 1756]. At a great supper t'other night at Lord Hertford's, if Lady Coventry was not the best-humoured creature in the world, I should have made her angry. She said, in a very vulgar accent, if she drank any more she should be *muckibus*! 'Lord,' said Lady Mary Coke, 'what is that?' – 'Oh!' I said, 'it is only Irish for sentimental.'

Even if Lord Coventry were 'silly in a wise way', there may have been something behind the wisdom when he coursed his wife round the table to remove her make-up. It may have had white lead in it. Her married life lasted only for eight years, before she had to pay the price of being beautiful. Her sister the Duchess was said to have consumption, but it has been suggested that her own disease was due to the cosmetics.

Poor Lady Coventry concluded her short race with the same attention to her looks. She lay constantly on a couch, with a pocket-glass in her hand; and when that told her how great the change was, she took to her bed the last fortnight, had no light in her room but the lamp of a tea-kettle, and at last took things in through the curtains of her bed, without suffering them to be undrawn. The mob, who never quitted curiosity about her, went, to the number of ten thousand, only to see her coffin. If she had lived to be ninety like Helen, I believe they would have thought that her wrinkles deserved an epic poem. Poor thing! how far from ninety! she was not eight-and-twenty! Adieu!

CHAPTER TEN

A Perfect Tragedy

SOMEBODY asked a Frenchman to describe the Duke of Newcastle, in 1745. This was the statesman who governed England for seven years, and who retired from office poorer than he came. The Frenchman fumbled for some time, muttering about '*un certain tatillonage*', and ended by suggesting that one ought to imagine a dead body, hanged in chains, which was always fidgeting to be hanged somewhere else.

Thomas Pelham Holles was a buffoon. A pompous, fussy, honest, ambitious but not avaricious nonentity, who lost half an hour every morning when he got up and chased it for the rest of the day – who was nicknamed Permis because he always said '*Est-il permis?*' before he addressed a remark to the King – it was his sheepish fate to be the butt of every rational being, and to be dismissed in the end, without having meant to do harm, forgotten, foolish, innocent, despicable, and still fidgeting to be hung somewhere else – so long as he might be hung in the Garter. The story of his standing on the great Duke of Cumberland's train, at the funeral of George II, is well known. Other stories were told of his persecution by the wits of the period:

The ball, at Bedford-house, on Monday, was very numerous and magnificent. The two Princes were there, deep hazard, and the Dutch deputies, who are a proverb for their dulness: they have brought with them a young Dutchman who is the richest man of Amsterdam. I am amazed Mr Yorke has not married him! But the delightful part of the night was the appearance of the Duke of Newcastle, who is veering round again, as it is time to betray Mr Pitt. The Duchess [of Bedford] was at the very upper end of the gallery, and though some of the Pelham court were there too, yet they shewed so little cordiality to this revival of connexion, that Newcastle had nobody to attend him but Sir Edward Montagu, who kept pushing him all up the gallery. From thence he went into the hazard room, and wriggled, and shuffled, and lisped, and winked, and spied, till he got behind the Duke of Cumberland, the Duke of Bedford, and Rigby; the first of whom did not deign to notice him; but he must come to it. You would have died to see Newcastle's pitiful and distressed figure, – nobody went near him: he tried to flatter people, but they were too busy to mind him: in short, he was quite disconcerted; his treachery used to be so sheathed in folly, that he was never out of countenance; but it is plain he grows old. To finish his confusion and anxiety, George Selwyn, Brand and I, went and stood near him, and in half whispers, that he might hear, said, 'Lord, how he is broke! how old he looks!' then I said, 'This room feels very cold: I believe there never was a fire in it.' Presently afterwards I said, 'Well, I'll not stay here; this room has been washed today.' In short, I believe we made him take a double dose of Gascoign's powder when he went home.

WALPOLE TO MONTAGU, 1759

There were several anecdotes about his farcical ability to be in the wrong place, as he was at the coronation of George III.

The Coronation is over: 'tis a more gorgeous sight than I imagined. I saw the procession and the Hall; but the return was in the dark. In the morning they had forgot the Sword of State, the chairs for King and Queen, and their canopies. They used the Lord Mayor's for the first, and made the last in the Hall: so they did not set forth till noon; and then, by a childish compliment to the King, reserved the illumination of the Hall till his entry; by which means they arrived like a funeral, nothing being discernible but the plumes of the Knights of the Bath, which seemed the hearse ... Of all the incidents of the day, the most diverting was what happened to the Queen. She had a retiring-chamber, with *all* conveniences, prepared behind the altar. She went thither – in the *most convenient* what found she but – the Duke of Newcastle!

WALPOLE TO CONWAY, 1761

It was this creature who was the first minister of England, and who was determined to remain in that position, when the Seven Years War began. The French were prepared, the English were not, and it was essential to the Duke that his ministry should remain in power. The French had invaded the English base of Minorca before he had noticed anything amiss; on the island there was an octogenarian governor, and half the officers of the garrison were on leave. Something had to be done, in fear of the Mob's resentment, so Admiral Byng was sent to stop the gap. The French were already ashore with an army, besieging the doting governor, and the Mediterranean was in the balance.

Admiral Byng was not exactly an impressive person. At all events, he was not flamboyant. He was a son of the great Admiral Lord Torrington, who had won the decisive naval battle of Cape Passero by mistake, and he had probably been oppressed by that tempestuous old tar. His expression, according to his nephew, was like the King of Prussia's, 'with the same round, smooth, unmeaning face, and the same little, mischievous nose'. He was subject to faintly comic accidents. 'Admiral Byng,' wrote his sister Sarah in 1750, 'thrown down in his park by a buck; now gone to Bath, and surprisingly recovered.' But he was a professional sailor who had been at sea since boyhood: he had taken an enemy ship in 1745: and he was no coward, for he had fought a duel to defend his honour.

Byng was dispatched to face the French admiral, with ships too few and too rotten, and with contradictory instructions. He was to relieve Minorca, but also to defend the naval dockyard of Gibraltar – which was in a state of disrepair – after he had passed it.

Until Rodney was to succeed in introducing the novel manoeuvre of 'breaking the line', the fighting tactics of the English fleet were simple. The admiral was expected to lay his capital ships in a direct line, parallel to the line of the enemy, and then each ship, one against one, was expected to sail down upon her adversary and blow her out of the water. There was a simple book of flag signals, by which the admiral might alter the movements of his fleet, with this end in view.

All ships of both fleets were motivated by air, so that no ship could sail against the wind that moved her. When two lines were placed in combat, the line which happened to be to the windward of the two possessed more power of manoeuvre than the other; for it could take the wind from the other's sails. Consequently it was an advantage to be on the windward side, and, before a battle, there was a vital competition for this position, which was called 'racing for the weather gage'.

When Byng, after confused negotiations at Gibraltar about his contradictory instructions, had sighted the French fleet off Minorca, he proceeded to race for the weather gage. He was willing to lay his foul bottoms ship to ship, against the French line.

His enemies were newly launched from Toulon, and their clean hulls gave them the legs of the encrusted English. They were also better gunned.

Byng's adversary, the Marquis de la Galissonière, was a talented commander. He knew that the unwished initiative lay with Byng. His own troops were already landed, and his duty was only to preserve their lines of communication. The English had two duties: to raise the siege and to protect Gibraltar. If Galissonière could keep himself 'in being', he would be doing all that was needed. Byng had to keep in being, and also to do something more.

In the last stages of laying the lines abreast of each other, one line of ships was accustomed to await the onslaught, while the possessor of the weather gage sailed down upon it. The attackers were compelled to make the last quarter mile 'end-on', while the defenders were in broadside. In the bow of a battleship there were only two guns, called bow-chasers, while the waiting line could bear with its whole armament.

Galissonière saw his opportunity. He would pretend to race for the weather gage, but would yield it to Byng. Then, with his fleet in line ahead, their broadsides bearing, he would lie-to and await the English.

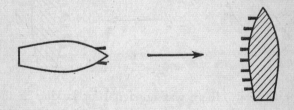

As they sailed down upon him, but before they came to close quarters, he would rake them with his full metal, while the English guns, except for the bow-chasers, could not be brought to bear. When they did reach close quarters, but before they were near enough to take his wind, he would use his superior speed to withdraw to a distance, would re-form his line, and would again await the suicidal attack. By repeating this manoeuvre *da capo*, he hoped to use his broadsides throughout the engagement, while his enemy's guns would never bear at all.

It was a measure of Byng's professional insight that he perceived these tactics before they were brought into action. He knew that Galissonière had the legs of him; he saw that the weather gage had been given on purpose; the rest followed in course, for a French fleet had been known to use the same tactics before. The secondary need to defend Gibraltar made it essential to preserve his fleet from suicide, from the pursuit of a faster enemy who could strike without waiting to be struck.

Byng decided on the spur of the moment to make use of an unorthodox manoeuvre called 'lasking'. A lasking ship was one which shouldered through the water on a crab-wise diagonal, at a slower speed, but with its broadside bearing:

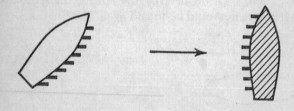

Unfortunately, there was no signal for lasking in the code book. He could only hope to institute the manoeuvre by example – and unfortunately an earlier movement of the fleets had placed his own squadron in the rear. There was a one-gun signal in the book, meaning 'Bear a point to starboard', which could be used as a hint to intelligent captains. His captains, however, were not intelligent, and they were excited. The unorthodox tactics were misunderstood. One captain, whose head was later taken off by a cannon ball, threw the movement into confusion. The two squadrons, of admiral and rear-admiral, fell foul of each other. Muddle and delay took place, under the guns of the French. The confused fleet, already much shattered, had scarcely been reduced to order, when Galissonière, as he had intended, withdrew, reformed, and awaited a second onslaught.

It was late in the day, too late to resume for the time being. That night a council of war on board the flag-ship, with the bugbear of Gibraltar at its back, decided unanimously to break off the action.

Angelo visited a warship after Lord Howe's victory in 1794 (the Glorious First of June) and from him we may extract a verbal picture of the conditions under which that council of war was probably held.

When we went below deck, the scene was truly frightful; on each side were hammocks on the floor, with numbers of dying and wounded; many of their comrades were seen praying to them, holding up the cross, and some appeared lifeless. At this moment I fancy I see their pale faces and black beards. Here great havoc must have been made, as the shot appeared, from the grooves on the deck, like that of a ploughshare on the earth, to have raked through the cabin, from stem to stern. Our curiosity did not last long; the smell, with the sight of the dying, and the groans of the wounded, soon put an end to our naval visit.

Such were the bare bones of a battle which lost Minorca, and which wrecked the Newcastle admini-stration. The miserable Duke, however, was a man who could hanker for authority to the last. In a desperate attempt to retain power, he proceeded to lay the blame on Byng: the blame for a war begun before the ministry was ready for it, for ships not clean nor properly manned, and for instructions from which it was im-possible to determine whether Minorca or Gibraltar had been the vital base. Grub Street writers were hired to blast the admiral's reputation. Mobs were suborned to howl for his death, singing

> Swing! Swing!
> Great Admiral Byng!

The fussy George II, with his foible for personal courage, was informed that his commander had been a coward. The octogenarian of Minorca was stifled with honours, much to his delight, after having stood the siege and capitulated in bed.

The wretched sacrifice was relieved of his command. He was haled home in disgrace, locked in a small room with a streaming cold and no assistance or conveniences, burnt in effigy, mocked by the Mob, and put up for court martial. The members of the court, like so many old tars, knew nothing of law. They were convinced of Byng's innocence, but they had been told that the fire-eating King would be furious if he were acquitted. They brought in a verdict which was intended to be a vote of censure, but which turned out to be a verdict of guilty. Their consciences smote them: they asked to be allowed to explain themselves to parliament: they broke down in the explanation. The great men of Europe did their utmost to save the victim. Pitt pleaded for him with the King, but was 'cut very short'. Lord Temple was so rude to his majesty on the same subject that he was never forgiven. Dr Johnson rallied to the rescue with his pen. Voltaire, who was later to make the bitter explanation that Byng had been shot '*pour encourager les autres*', wrote a testimonial from Paris. Galissonière himself spoke to the admiral's bravery. The fabulous de Richelieu, also an enemy, forwarded a testimonial from France. '*Je vous assure que tout ce que j'ai vu et su de lui ne devait tourner qu'à sa gloire.*' Rear-Admiral West, Byng's second-in-command, who had been commended by the court, resigned his flag. But red-tape, Permis, the guttural King, and the raving Mob, were not to be turned back.

Meanwhile, the Admiral of the Blue, a solid, not unkindly, ugly and unimportant figure of middle height, who had been popular with his men, had lost hope. Everything from the start had been a muddle. It had been an accumulating confusion which he was too tired to explain. The Fighting Instructions, the behaviour of his captains, the battle itself, the imbecile court martial, all had produced a tangle too complicated to be unravelled. Even the attempt to save the Administration, for which he was to be sacrificed, had gone agley. He did, however, desire to defend his honour. He was willing to be shot, but he wanted not to leave the reputation of a coward. When a tactful friend came to him on board the *Monarque*, where he was waiting for the firing squad, and asked jestingly, 'Which of us is the tallest?' he replied, 'Why this ceremony? I know what it means: let the man come and measure me for my coffin.' He offered to open his shirt for the bullets, to show that he was not afraid of them. He begged to be allowed to give the order for his own volley, and that he should not be blindfold. By a strange quirk, on the morning of his execution, he took his usual draught for scurvy.

He had written to Sarah two days before his execution.

March 12, 1757

My dear, dear Sister, – I can only with my last breath thank you over and over again for all your endeavours to serve me in my present situation. All has proved fruitless, but nothing wanting in you that could be done. God forever bless you is the sincere prayers of your most affect. Bro.

J. BYNG

Enclosed I send you a receipt for Bro. Edward's legacy, which you will do me the favour to accept of as a small token of my affection for you.

A few minutes before he was shot, he handed a paper to the Marshal:

ON BOARD HIS MAJESTY'S SHIP MONARQUE, IN PORTSMOUTH HARBOUR. March 14, 1757

A few moments will now deliver me from the virulent persecution, and frustrate the further malice of my enemies – nor need I envy them a life subject to the sensations my injuries and the injustice done me must create. Persuaded I am, justice will be done to my reputation hereafter. The manner and cause of raising and keeping up the popular clamor and prejudice against me, will be seen thro'. I shall be considered (as I now perceive myself) a victim destined to divert the indignation and resentment of an injured and deluded people from the proper objects. My enemies themselves must even now think me innocent. Happy for me at this my last moment, that I know my own innocence, and am conscious that no part of my country's misfortunes can be owing to me. I heartily wish the shedding of my blood may contribute to the happiness and service of my country, but cannot resign my just claim to a faithful discharge of my duty, according to the best of my judgement, and the utmost extension of my ability for His Majesty's honor and my country's service. I am sorry that my endeavours were not attended with more success, and that the armament under my command proved too weak to succeed in an expedition of such moment. Truth has prevailed over calumny and falsehood, and justice has wiped off the ignominious stain of my supposed want of personal courage, or disaffection. My heart acquits me of these crimes, but who can be presumptuously sure of his own judgement? If my crime is an error in judgement, or differing in opinion from my judges, and if yet the error in judgement should be on their side, God forgive them, as I do, and may the distress of their minds and uneasiness of their consciences, which in justice to me they have represented, be relieved and subside as my resentment has done. The Supreme Judge sees all hearts and motives, to Him I must submit the justice of my cause.

J. BYNG

He said, that being acquitted of cowardice, and being persuaded on the coolest reflection that he had acted for the best, and should act so again, he was not unwilling to suffer. He desired to be shot on the quarter-deck, not where common malefactors were; came out at twelve, sat down in a chair, for he would not kneel, and refused to have his face covered, that his countenance might shew whether he feared death; but being told that it might frighten his executioners, he submitted, gave the signal at once, received one shot through the head, another through the heart, and fell. Do cowards live or die thus? Can that man want spirit who only fears to terrify his executioners? Has the aspen Duke of Newcastle lived thus?

WALPOLE TO MANN, 1757

Byng was fifty-three at death. He was buried at Southill, Bedfordshire, with this inscription on his monument:

TO THE PERPETUAL DISGRACE OF PUBLIC JUSTICE
THE HONBLE JOHN BYNG, ESQRE
ADMIRAL OF THE FLEET
FELL A MARTYR TO POLITICAL PERSECUTION
MARCH 14TH IN THE YEAR 1757, WHEN
BRAVERY AND LOYALTY
WERE INSUFFICIENT SECURITIES FOR THE
LIFE AND HONOUR
OF A NAVAL OFFICER

Aristotle defined tragedy as an action in which some person of high station should fall, through an error or frailty, and should thus purge the emotions of the audience, by pity and by fear. Byng's station had been high, for his father had been the famous and fertile Lord

Torrington. His fall might have been due to an error, though it had been due to no crime. Walpole wrote to Sir Horace Mann on 17 March 1757:

Admiral Byng's tragedy was completed on Monday – a perfect tragedy.

CHAPTER ELEVEN

The Church Militant

IT has become an aphorism among scientists that great discoveries are seldom due to the efforts of a single person. Darwin's theory of natural selection was anticipated by Alfred Russel Wallace, before Darwin was ready to publish, and the *Origin of Species* began with a list which mentioned dozens of embyro evolutionists, who had preceded them both. The earliest in that list were Geoffrey Saint-Hilaire, who published *c.* 1795, Dr Erasmus Darwin, the writer's eccentric grandfather, 1794, Lamarck, 1801, and apparently Goethe. But these were far from being the first Darwinians.

If it had not been for a fit of laughing [wrote Walpole in 1773], I really should have lost my *sang-froid* t'other morning. My Phoenician, Irish, antiquarian friend, kept me two hours with a new system of the Mosaic creation, which he has discovered to be the true meaning of the book of Genesis. He told me that this world had originally been all mud, and was inhabited by a set of animals proper to such a quagmire; that it was the natural progress of things, and that there were many orbs round the sun now changing from water to earth. Lord! said I, a little fired, why you talk as if there were several worlds hung out to dry. Instead of being angry, he replied gravely, and glad to find I was so apt a disciple, *Just that,* – no, I own, I could then keep my countenance no longer. . . .

In the same year, the interesting and unusual Lord Monboddo had begun to publish his work on the origin of language, in which he maintained that the orang-outang was related to human beings, and claimed, to the amusement of Boswell and of Dr Johnson, that our own species possessed tails.

Dr Johnson said, 'It is a pity to see Lord Monboddo publish such notions as he has done; a man of sense, and of so much elegant learning. There would be little in a fool doing it; we should only laugh; but when a wise man does it, we are sorry. Other people have strange notions, but they conceal them. If they have tails, they hide them; but Monboddo is as jealous of his tail as a squirrel.'

Similar ideas had been floating about since the seventeen-twenties, when Elijah Fenton published a couplet which inverted the modern sequence:

> Foes to the tribe from which they trace their clan,
> As monkeys draw their pedigree from man.

The predominant religious texture of the eighteenth century was that of belief, and the Age of Scandal was perhaps the last period of English history in which persons of the highest education could subscribe to the Thirty-nine Articles without hypocrisy. Scholars as learned as Dr Johnson could be as bigoted in their Christianity as George III – although, incidentally, the learning of Johnson was by no means on a par with that of the high scholars like Gibbon or Porson – and philosophers as acute as Berkeley could be bishops.

The gradations of belief were shaded between the definite agnosticism of the few and great, through the doubts of self-dramatizing people who called themselves *esprits forts* or the 'deism' of aristocrats like Shaftesbury, Bolingbroke, Tolland, Tindal, Collins, and Walpole, to the stout conservative Christianity of the middle classes and to the Wesleyan revivalism, or quakerism, or sheer ignorance and 'ranting' of the gin-fed Mob.

Agnostics included people like the philosopher Hume, who had removed the Ego to which Berkeley had reduced the Universe by way of the senses; Gibbon, who knew too much about the comparative history of religions to be a devotee of any one of them; Baskerville, the designer of the famous type, an interesting man who was buried in his own garden under a stone which said,

Stranger,
beneath this stone, in *unconsecrated* ground,
a friend to the liberties of mankind directed his body to be inurn'd.
May the example contribute to emancipate thy mind
from the idle fears of *Superstition*
and the wicked arts of Priesthood.

There was also John Fransham, who decided that God was Space; and possibly the early scientists like Tom Paine, Dr Darwin, Messenger Monsey, and Monboddo.

The sages provoked a fervid hostility from all right-thinking people. 'And as to Hume,' exclaimed Johnson with fury, '– a man who has so much conceit as to tell all mankind that they have been bubbled for ages, and he is the wise man who sees better than they, – a man who has so little scrupulosity as to venture to oppose those principles which have been thought necessary to human happiness ... He added "*something much too rough*", both as to Mr Hume's head and heart, which I suppress.' 'A wickeder heart than Hume's,' said Warburton, 'and more determined to do public mischief, I think I never knew.' Boswell, on the other hand, as usual much more sensible than his superiors, was surprised to perceive that Hume was a charming person. 'Besides, I always lived on good terms with Mr Hume, though I have frankly told him, I was not clear that it was right in me to keep company with him.'

The *esprits forts*, who were often young noblemen in revolt against established decency without the backing of scholarship for a foundation, later found their best voice perhaps in Byron – who wrote, in 1811, a letter of mingled nonsense and penetration, that was memorable for at least one sentence about immortality:

One remark, and I have done; the basis of your religion is *injustice*; the *Son* of *God*, the *pure*, the *immaculate*, the *innocent*, is sacrificed for the *Guilty*. This proves *His* heroism; but no more does away *man's* guilt than a schoolboy's volunteering to be flogged for another would exculpate the dunce from negligence, or preserve him from the Rod. You degrade the Creator, in the first place, by making Him a begetter of children; and in the next you convert Him into a Tyrant over an immaculate and injured Being, who is sent into existence to suffer death for the benefit of some millions of Scoundrels, who, after all, seem as likely to be damned as ever. As to miracles, I agree with Hume that it is more probable men should *lie* or be *deceived*, than that things out of the course of Nature should so happen. Mahomet wrought miracles, Brothers the prophet had *proselytes*, and so would Breslaw the conjuror, had he lived in the time of Tiberius.

Besides, I trust that God is not a Jew, but the God of all mankind; and as you allow that a virtuous Gentile may be saved, you do away the necessity of being a Jew or a Christian.

I do not believe in any revealed religion, because no religion is revealed: and if it pleases the Church to damn me for not allowing a *nonentity*, I throw myself on the mercy of the '*Great First Cause, least understood*', who must do what is most proper; though I conceive He never made anything to be tortured in another life, whatever it may be in this. I will neither read *pro* nor *con*. God would have made His will known without books, considering how very few could read them when Jesus of Nazareth lived, had it been His pleasure to ratify any peculiar mode of worship. As to your immortality, if people are to live why die? And our carcases, which are to rise again, are they worth raising?

The 'deists', a branch of these strong spirits to whom perhaps Byron might more properly be said to have belonged, were of opinion that some First Cause must exist, on the argument that 'somebody must have made the world', but that no revealed religion could be trusted to tell them about it. Voltaire informed a certain Mr Higginson that he himself was a Deist, 'adding, so were most of the noblemen in France and in England'. This section, to which Horace Walpole and others of the educated aristocracy and of the rakes like Wilkes or Queensberry adhered, supposed that the Church of England was beneficial in its restraining effect upon the Mob, and they therefore encouraged its application to others, while retaining an amused detachment themselves.

'*Quel ton!*' observed the Maréchale de Luxembourg, on reading the Bible, '*Quel effroyable ton! Ah, Madame, quel dommage que le Saint Esprit eût aussi peu de goût!*'

The aristocracy was, however, Christian politically and by instinctive prejudice, and probably even Queensberry would have been deeply shocked by the opinions of a modern biologist.

Deists, *esprits forts*, and ahnostics, all lumped together, might have made up less than one-hundredth of 1 per cent of the population.

The remainder were Christians of various kinds; many of them were clergymen; and the Established Church in the eighteenth century was an exciting institution. The sinecures and place-hunting of Parliament were duplicated in the life of religion; its prizes were as great and the competitors were as practical. Bishop Chandler was accused of having paid £9,000 for the see of Durham. Trollope's picture of the Warden at Barchester was no fiction.

I saw St Cross, too [wrote Gray to the Rev. James Brown in 1764], the almshouse of Noble Poverty (so it was called), founded by Henry de Blois and Cardinal Beaufort. It maintains nine decayed footmen, and a master (Chancellor Hoadly), who has 800L. a-year out of it.

Plural livings were common. Dignitaries could be bishops in one diocese, deans in another, and vicars in a third. The Archbishop of Canterbury had £25,000 a year, the Bishop of London £20,000. Successful clergymen constituted a monied aristocracy who ate and drank well. The Rev. Samuel Ogden considered a goose to be a silly bird: it was too big for one dish and not enough for two. Mason was ashamed to admit that he could only manage one bottle of port at a sitting. 'The poor,' said a prelate in the House of Lords, 'have nothing to do with the laws but to obey them.'

At the end of this period, according to Sydney Smith, there were 10,478 benefices: of which 297 were worth only £40 per annum; 1629 were worth £75 per annum, and 1602 rose to £125. On 4606 of these livings there were no houses fit for habitation. In short, while Canterbury enjoyed his plum of £25,000 and two palaces, 3,528 of his clergy – one-third of the total number – were below the level of farmers, and the average income of the Church, if equally divided, would have worked out at £250 for each minister, bishops included. Sir William Scott's estimate was even lower. According to him, out of 11,700 livings, 'there are 6,000 under 80L. *per annum*; many of those, 20L., 30L., and some as low as 2L. or 3L. *per annum*'. Sydney Smith himself calculated that 'till thirty years of age I never received a farthing from the Church, then 50L. per annum for two years – then nothing for ten years – then 500L. per annum, increased for two or three years to 800L. till, in my grand climacteric, I was made Canon of St Paul's;

and before that period, I had built a Parsonage-house with farm offices for a large farm, which cost me 4000L., and had reclaimed another from ruins for 2000L.'

It was at this point, however, that the mind of this particular Canon of St Paul's performed its usual volte-face. The state of affairs, he proceeded to explain, was right and reasonable. If the revenues of the Church were to be redistributed, so that everybody had £250 a year, then educated gentlemen would no longer become clergymen. 'Who would go into the Church and spend 1,200L. or 1,500L. upon his education, if such were the highest remuneration he could ever look to? At present, men are tempted into the Church by the prizes of the Church, and bring into that Church a great deal of capital, which enables them to live in decency, supporting themselves, not with the money of the public, but with their own money, which, but for this temptation, would have been carried into some retail trade. The offices of the Church would then fall down to men little less coarse and ignorant than agricultural labourers – the clergyman of the parish would soon be seen in the squire's kitchen.' It was better to leave things as they were. A proposed pillage of Cathedral and College dignitaries would only amount, 'divided among all the benefices in England, to about 5L. 12s. 6½d. per man', which 'would not stop an hiatus in a cassock, and would drive out of the parochial Church ten times as much as it brought into it'. It was wiser to regard the situation as a lottery, possessing great prizes. The revenues of Christ were too small to support his ministers decently, so they must simply take the affair as a sweepstake. Innocents would then enter, under the delusion that they might themselves draw the winning number of Cantuar, and religion would be served by independent gentlemen of education and private means.

To the lottery, then, the clerics of the Age of Scandal resorted, and the barefacedness with which they ran for the prizes, not without dust and heat, was in keeping with the sincerity of an admirable age. Paley, of the *Evidences of Christianity*, had wished at the University to defend the thesis 'Aeternitas poenarum contradicit divinis attributis'. The Master of his college objecting, he inserted a 'non', and defended that. Later, when the young Pitt attended the University Church, Paley suggested for a text in the sermon: 'There is a lad here who hath five barley loaves and two small fishes; but what are they among so many?'

The old man [wrote the Rev. William Mason to Gray in 1761] was really dying when I wrote to you from Stilton; but, in spite of an added fever and fistuala, he still holds out, has had strength to undergo two operations, and is in hopes of a perfect recovery. However, if he ever does die, I am now sure of succeeding him, and I find the object of much more importance than I first thought, for, one year with another, by fines &c., the preferment is good 230L. per annum.

Your friend Dr Plumptre [wrote Gray to Mason, referring to the President of Queens', who also possessed the livings of Wimpole and Whadden, and who was later to add a prebendal stall at Norwich] has lately sat for his picture to Wilson. The motto, in large letters (the measure of which he himself prescribed), is 'Non magna loquimur, sed vivimus': i.e. 'We don't say much, but we hold good livings.'

Nichols records the epitaph of Mrs Elizabeth Bate, relict of the Rev. Richard Bate, 'a woman of unaffected piety and exemplary virtue':

> She was honourably descended
> And by means of her Alliance to

The illustrious family of Stanhope
She had the merit to obtain
For her husband and children
Twelve several employments
In Church and State.

Sometimes the winners of prizes were a trifle un-expected, as was the case with Dr Lancelot Blackburne, Walpole's 'jolly old Archbishop of York, who had all the manners of a man of quality, though he had been a *buccaneer*', and who was said to have kept a seraglio at the Palace. A later Bishop of Norwich was believed to be his natural son.

Sometimes the race for preferment was neck and neck.

On the 18th of January, 1805, died, after a protracted ill-ness, Dr John Moore, Archbishop of Canterbury. As it was more than conjected by well-informed persons that Pitt was bent on elevating to the primacy his old tutor, and after-wards secretary, Dr Tomline, Bishop of Lincoln and Dean of St Paul's, and, on the other hand, as it was whispered that the King was no less anxious for the advancement of Dr Manners Sutton, Bishop of Norwich and Dean of Windsor, a good deal of interest was excited as to the result among the friends of the rival prelates. ...

The King received a message from Pitt that Archbishop Moore was dead, and that he would wait upon his Majesty the next morning. The King, suspecting the cause, ordered his horse, and rode over to Bishop Sutton, then residing at Windsor. He found he was at dinner with some friends, and sent in the servant to say a gentleman wished to speak with him. The Bishop said immediately he could not go; but something in the servant's manner made him change his determination. When he came out, he found the King standing in a little dressing room, near the hall door. The King took him by both hands. 'My Lord Archbishop of Canterbury (he said), I wish you joy. Not a word: go back to your guests.' ...

On Pitt's arrival next day ... Lord Sidmouth told Dean Milman that he believed such strong language had rarely ever passed between a Sovereign and his Minister.

JESSE

Sometimes the strain of competition was too much for those of weaker nerves. Florizel's flogging tutor Dr Arnold stood the course till he had achieved the Canonry of Windsor and the Archdeaconry of Lichfield, but then ran mad, and ever afterwards walked about his house in a mitre.

No wonder the successful prelates were proud and pompous. No wonder they disapproved of penniless demagogues like Wesley and were pleased by a church bell, cast during the eighteenth century in defiance of that preacher, which bore the noble inscription: 'Hurrah for the Church of England and down with Enthusiasm.' No wonder that Bishop Dawes, on being asked if he had seen a late eclipse of the moon, replied with grandeur: 'No, Madam, but my chaplain did; *I* saw the eclipse of the sun.'

While his Lordship consumed his port with a right pride in himself and a due sense of God's mercies through Christ, the country clergyman, like Parson Adams, lived in penury, the toady chaplain employed as the tutor to a noble family waited for preferment with his tongue hanging out, and the curate related to a bishop, as Sydney Smith remarked, spent his time like the sloth which hung from a tree 'in a state of suspense'.

But if the struggle for power were internecine, yet the ecclesiastical world was saved from a great strain: it was spared the necessity of averting its mind from the discoveries soon to be promulgated by Darwin. England was solidly Protestant: it was fashionable, usual, nearly unquestionable that the Thirty-nine Articles should be accepted without examination as 'articles of peace'. Consequently, with the burdens of modern biology not yet imposed upon their minds, the clergy were able to offer a healthier and franker companionship to their fellow men than was to be possible in the twentieth century. 'Frank' was sometimes a meiosis. They wrote, *sans gêne*, about the bodily functions and the harlots of their acquaintance. They betrayed few traces of surprise when their parishioners decamped to the *bagula*. Their letters, as published, were peppered with asterisks. 'Our friend Foljambe has resided in college, and persevered in the ways of godliness till about ten days ago, when he disappeared, and no one knows whether he has gone a hunting or a * * * * .'

Occasionally they stepped a little too far, and were hanged for forgery like Dr Dodd, or for shooting Lord Sandwich's mistress like the Rev. James Hackman, or for murdering their pupils like the Rev. Thomas Hunter; but on the whole their deportment was as correct as their language was unhampered. It was an age in which the oratory of the pulpit, the sermon, was relished as oratory, in the same way as were the declamations of Garrick on the boards or the speeches of the playwright Sheridan in Parliament. So long as these graces were achieved, and an outward propriety offered as an example to the plebs, the beneficed clergyman remained a gentleman outside his pulpit, and claimed the privileges of such. This was the background against which the Rev. Laurence Sterne, whose sermons were admired by Gray and whom Society regarded as an amusingly shocking but by no means as a monstrous parson, either pursued his own humiliating amours, or disclosed the details of the night on which Tristram Shandy was conceived, or related the curious story of the latter's accident with the sash-window. The morals of Sterne, though deprecated in many quarters, were not officially considered as scandalous to his cloth, and, although the King was cross with the Archbishop of Canterbury for holding routs at Lambeth Palace, no objection seems to have been raised by others to the conviviality of a certain Rev. Mr Porter, vicar of East Hoathly, which was recorded in the diary of bibulous but remorseful Thomas Turner, shopkeeper of that parish:

1757. Feb. 22 (Wednesday) About four P.M. I walked down to Whyly. We played at bragg the first part of the even. After ten we went to supper on four boiled chicken, four boiled ducks, minced veal, sausages, cold roast goose, chicken pasty, and ham. Our company, Mr and Mrs Porter, Mr and Mrs Coates, Mrs Atkins, Mrs Hicks, Mr Piper and wife, Joseph Fuller and wife, Dame Durrant, myself and wife, and Mr French's family. After supper our behaviour was far from that of serious, harmless mirth; it was downright obstreperous, mixed with a great deal of folly and stupidity. Our diversion was dancing or jumping about, without a violin or any music, singing of foolish healths, and drinking all the time as fast as it could be well poured down; and the parson of the parish was one among the mixed multitude. If conscience declares right from wrong, as doubtless it sometimes does, mine is one that I may say is soon offended; for, I must say, I am always very uneasy at such behaviour, thinking it not like the behaviour of the primitive Christians, which I imagine was more in conformity to our Saviour's gospel. Nor would I be thought to be either a cynic or a stoic, but let social improving discourse pass round the company. About three o'clock, finding myself to have about as much liquor as would do me good, I slipt away unobserved, leaving my wife to make my excuse. Though I was very far from sober, I came home, thank God, very safe and well, without even tumbling; and Mr French's servant brought my wife home at ten minutes past five.

23. (Thursday) This morning about six o'clock just as my wife was got to bed, we was awaked by Mrs Porter, who pretended she wanted some cream of tartar; but as soon as my wife got out of bed, she vowed she should come down. She found Mr Porter, Mr Fuller and his wife, with a lighted candle, and part of a bottle of wine and a glass. The next thing was to have me downstairs, which being apprized of, I fastened my door. Up stairs they came, and threatened to break it open; so I ordered the boys to open it, when they poured into my room; and, as modesty forbid me to get out of bed, so I refrained; but their immodesty permitted them to draw me out of bed, as the common phrase is, topsy turvy; but, however, at the intercession of Mr Porter, they permitted me to put on my *******, and instead of my upper cloaths, they gave me time to put on my wife's petticoats; and in this manner they made me dance, without shoes and stockings, until they had emptied the bottle of wine, and also a bottle of my beer.

About three o'clock in the afternoon they found their way to their respective homes, beginning to be a little serious, and, in my opinion, ashamed of their stupid enterprise and drunken perambulation. Now, let any one call in reason to his assistance, and seriously reflect on what I have before recited, and they will join with me in thinking that the precepts delivered from the pulpit on Sunday, tho' delivered with the greatest ardour, must lose a great deal of their efficacy by such examples.

March 5 (Sunday) We had as good a sermon as I ever heard Mr Porter preach, it being against swearing.

7 (Tuesday) We continued drinking like horses, as the vulgar phrase is, and singing till many of us were very drunk, and then we went to dancing and pulling wigs, caps, and hats; and thus we continued in this frantic manner, behaving more like mad people than they that profess the name of Christians. Whether this is consistent to the wise saying of Solomon, let any one judge: Wine is a mocker, strong drink is raging, and he that is deceived thereby is not wise.

10 Supped at Mr Porter's, where the same scene took place, with the exception that there was no swearing and no ill words, by reason of which Mr Porter calls it innocent mirth, but I in opinion differ much therefrom.

11 (Saturday). At home all day. Very piteous.

It may be noticed that Thomas Turner must have been touched with the new heresy of Methodism, possibly because he was a shopkeeper; for otherwise he would never have bandied texts on the conduct of so convivial a parson. It may have been as a punishment for his dissent that he was made to dance in the petticoats.

Among the lower classes, Methodism was already beginning to substitute the bogy God of the Victorians for the Arch-archbishop of a brighter epoch. The dismal and humourless fanaticism of Wesley – who preached 42,400 sermons during his ministry – was undermining the bishops in their wigs and bands, and the abominable proletariat had begun to go a-whoring after the strange and gloomy gods of guilt and shame. The original Quakers had really quaked, and Wesley's diary records with pious satisfaction in 1761 that 'I was scarce come into the room where a few believers were met together when one began to tremble exceedingly, and soon after sunk to the floor'. Sydney Smith, who complained on his death-bed of being so weak that 'I verily believe, if the knife were put into my hand, I should not have strength or energy enough to stick it into a Dissenter', made a collection of cuttings from Methodist papers.

The following we consider to be one of the most shocking histories we ever read. God only knows how many such scenes take place in the gloomy annals of Methodism:

A young man, of the name of S— C—, grandson to a late eminent Dissenting minister, and brought up by him, came to reside at K——g, about the year 1803. He attended at the Baptist place of worship, not only on the Lord's day, but frequently at the weekday lectures and prayer-meetings. He was supposed by some to be seriously inclined; but his opinion of himself was, that he had never experienced that divine change, without which no man can be saved.

However that might be, there is reason to believe he had been for some years under powerful convictions of his miserable condition as a sinner. In June 1806, these convictions were observed to increase, and that in a more than common degree. From that time he went into no company; but, when he was not at work, kept in his chamber, where he was employed in singing plaintive hymns, and bewailing his lost and perishing state.

He had about him several religious people; but could not be induced to open his mind to them, or to impart to any one the cause of his distress. Whether this contributed to increase it or not, it did increase, till his health was greatly affected by it, and he was scarcely able to work at his business.

While he was at meeting on Lord's day, September 14th, he was observed to labour under very great emotion of mind, especially when he heard the following words. 'Sinner, if you die without an interest in Christ, you will sink into the regions of eternal death.'

On the Saturday evening following, he intimated to the mistress of the house where he lodged, that some awful judgement was about to come upon him; and as he should not be able to be at meeting next day, requested that an attendant might be procured to stay with him. She replied, that she would herself stay at home, and wait upon him; which she did.

On the Lord's day, he was in great agony of mind. His mother was sent for, and some religious friends visited him; but all was of no avail. That night was a night dreadful beyond all conception. The horror which he endured brought on all the symptoms of raging madness.

He desired the attendants not to come near him, lest they should be burnt. He said that 'the bed-curtains were in flames, – that he smelt the brimstone, – that devils were come to fetch him, – that there was no hope for him, for that he had sinned against light and conviction, and that he would certainly go to hell'. It was with difficulty he could be kept in bed.

An apothecary being sent for, as soon as he entered the house, and heard his dreadful howlings, he inquired if he had not been bitten by a mad dog. His appearance, likewise, seemed to justify such a suspicion, his countenance resembling that of a wild beast more than that of a man.

Though he had no feverish heat, yet his pulse beat above 150 in a minute. To abate the *mania*, a quantity of blood was taken from him, a blister was applied, his head was shaved, cold water was copiously poured over him, and fox-glove was administered. By these means his fury was abated; but his mental agony continued, and all the symptoms of madness which his bodily strength, thus reduced, would allow, till the following Thursday. On that day he seemed to have recovered his reason, and to be calm in his mind. In the evening he sent for the apothecary; and wished to speak with him by himself. The latter, on his coming, desired every one to leave the room, and thus addressed him: 'C—, have you not something on your mind?' 'Ay,' answered he, '*that is it*!' He then acknowledged that, early in the month of June, he had gone to a fair in the neighbourhood, in company with a number of wicked young men: that they drank at a public-house together till he was in a measure intoxicated; and that from thence they went into other company, where he was criminally connected with a harlot. 'I have been a miserable creature,' continued he, 'ever since; but during the last three days and three nights, I have been in a state of desperation.' He intimated to the apothecary, that he could not bear to tell this story to his minister: 'But,' said he, 'do you inform him that I shall not die in despair; for light has broken in upon me; I have been led to the great Sacrifice for sin, and I now hope in Him for salvation.'

From this time his mental distress ceased, his countenance became placid, and his conversation, instead of being taken up as before with fearful exclamations concerning devils and the wrath to come, was now confined to the dying love of Jesus! The apothecary was of opinion, that if his strength had not been so much exhausted, he would now have been in a state of religious transport. His nervous system, however, had received such a shock, that his recovery was doubtful; and it seemed certain, that if he did recover, he would sink into a state of idiocy. He survived this interview but a few days.

Evening Magazine

To so merry a dignitary as Sydney, writing in 1808, the ludicrous transports of the pleasure-haters were insufferable and ungentlemanly. It will be remembered that it was to a Methodist that the proud Duchess of Argyll had compared poor Bozzy, when she wanted to be rude. Sydney himself was 'quite sure that happiness will be destroyed, reason degraded, sound religion banished from the world; and that when fanaticism becomes too foolish and too prurient to be endured ... it will be succeeded by a long period of the grossest immorality, atheism and debauchery'. He had been a Whig all his life, a political shade which might now correspond to Socialism, but he could not stomach the new God. He dipped his pen in irony and scorn, to scotch the scandal with quotations – consoling himself by inventing cutting headlines, to suit the Methodist text. It was the idea that God should be expected to interfere in the pettiest affairs that hurt him most.

An interference respecting Cards.
'A clergyman not far distant from the spot on which these

lines were written, was spending an evening – not in his closet wrestling with his Divine Master for the communication of that grace which is so peculiarly necessary for the faithful discharge of the ministerial function, – not in his study searching the sacred oracles of divine truth for materials wherewith to prepare for his public exercises and feed the flock under his care, – not in pastoral visits to that flock, to inquire into the state of their souls, and endeavour, by his pious and affectionate conversation, to conciliate their esteem, and promote their edification, but at the *card table*.' After stating that when it was his turn to deal, he dropt down dead, 'It is worthy of remark (says the writer), that within a very few years this was the third character in the neighbourhood which had been summoned from the card-table to the bar of God.'

Evening Magazine, p. 262

Interference respecting Swearing, – a Bee the instrument.
A young man is stung by a bee, upon which he buffets the bees with his hat, uttering at the same time the most dreadful oaths and imprecations. In the midst of his fury, one of these little combatants stung him upon the tip of that unruly member (his tongue), which was then employed in blaspheming his Maker. Thus can the Lord engage one of the meanest of his creatures in reproving the bold transgressor who dares to take his name in vain.

Evening Magazine, p. 363

Interference with respect to David Wright, who was cured of Atheism and Scrofula by one sermon of Mr Coles.
This case is too long to quote in the language and with the evidence of the writers. The substance of it is what our title implies. – David Wright was a man with scrofulous legs and atheistical principles; – being with difficulty persuaded to hear one sermon from Mr Coles, he limped to the church in extreme pain, and arrived there after great exertions; – during church time he was entirely converted, walked home with the greatest ease, and never after experienced the slightest return of scrofula or infidelity.

The aristocratic attitude of the *poco-curante* to all these religious emotions was summed up by the villainous Thurlow, who, as Lord Chancellor, told a deputation of Nonconformists: 'I'm against you, by God. I am for the Established Church, damme! Not that I have any more regard for the Established Church than for any other Church, but because it is established. And if you can get your damned religion established, I'll be for that too!'

It is doubtful whether even establishment would have reconciled Thurlow to the lowest of religious classes then existing – the Ranters, from whom the other dissenting branches may possibly have sprung. These uneducated and generally insane enthusiasts formed a floating sub-normal who were willing to believe in anything that came along: in Joanna Southcott (1750–1814) as the new Virgin Mary, or in Mary Tofts as the mother of dismembered rabbits. They derived from fanatics of the previous century: from people like Reeve and Muggleton (1609–98), who believed that heaven was six miles away; like Abiezer Coppe (1619–72), who claimed to have baptized seven thousand persons and who preached stark naked; like Roger Crab (1621–80), who ate nothing but dock leaves and grass; like John Smith (d. 1612), who baptized himself; or like Thomas Tany (fl. 1649–55), who preferred to circumcise himself, had fits, sentenced Reeve 'to eternal damnation' in writing, and tried to fight his way into the House of Commons with a rusty sword. In the Age of Scandal their more amusing representatives were Samuel Best, who diagnosed the diseases of his followers by licking the palms of their hands and drank nothing but gin and rhubarb; and John Finlayson, who explained that the earth was a perfect sphere, 'not shaped like a garden turnip, as the Newtonians make it', that the sun was 'very different from anything we can make here below', and that the stars were 'oval-shaped immense masses of frozen water, with their largest ends foremost'.

CHAPTER TWELVE

The Learned Bargee

ONE day, probably in 1715, a little boy was making his way from school. Somebody was usually sent to fetch him, but on this occasion the conductor had not arrived. In 1715 the child would have been six years old.

He set out by himself, though he was then so near-sighted, that he was obliged to stoop down on his hands and knees to take a view of the kennel [gutter], before he ventured to step over it. His schoolmistress, afraid that he might miss his way, or fall into the kennel, or be run over by a cart, followed him at some distance. He happened to turn about and perceive her. Feeling her careful attention as an insult to his manliness, he ran back to her in a rage, and beat her, as well as his strength would permit.

This child – who had scrofula, one good eye, an inherited melancholia, St Vitus's dance, no money, and other disabilities – emerged from penury and Grub Street about forty years later, as the author of the first English Dictionary. He was finally buried in Westminster Abbey with a simple inscription:

SAMUEL JOHNSON LLD
Obiit xii die Decembris
Anno Domini
MDCCLXXXIV
Aetatis suae LXXV.

As an author, Johnson's fame was, to tell the truth, scarcely more than contemporary; for it depended upon *novelty of style*, in an age which loved personal novelties like the clothes of the later Brummell. To them, the not-ungraceful antithetical balancing feats with which he wrote of 'amorous propensities' rather than of 'love' were new and strange. As a lexicographer, he was of importance. As a conversationalist, the equivalent of our modern 'brains trust' – who would have been lost without the microphone of Boswell – he was of the first rank. It seems impossible to say anything about him in this capacity, except in the words of his devoted biographer.

... while talking or even musing as he sat in his chair, he commonly held his head to one side towards his right shoulder, and shook it in a tremulous manner, moving his body backwards and forwards, and rubbing his left knee in the same direction, with the palm of his hand. In the intervals of articulating he made various sounds with his mouth, sometimes as if ruminating, or what is called chewing the cud, sometimes giving a half whistle, sometimes making his tongue play backwards from the roof of his mouth, as if clucking like a hen, and sometimes protruding it against his upper gums in front, as if pronouncing quickly under his breath, *too, too, too*: all this accompanied sometimes with a thoughtful look, but more frequently with a smile. Generally when he had concluded a period, in the course of a dispute, by which time he was a good deal exhausted by violence and vociferation, he used to blow out his breath like a whale. This I suppose was a relief to his lungs; and seemed in him to be a contemptuous mode of expression, as if he had made the arguments of his opponent fly like chaff before the wind.

When he walked the streets [wrote Kearsley], what with the constant roll of his head, and the concomitant motion of his body, he appeared to make his way by that motion, independent of his feet.

His figure was large and well-formed, and his countenance of the cast of an ancient statue; yet his appearance was rendered strange and somewhat uncouth by convulsive cramps, by the scars of that distemper which it was once imagined the royal touch could cure, and by a slovenly mode of dress. He had the use only of one eye; yet so much does mind govern and even supply the deficiency of organs, that his visual perceptions, as far as they extended, were uncommonly quick and accurate. So morbid was his temperament that he never knew the natural joy of a free and vigorous use of his limbs; when he walked, it was like the struggling gait of one in fetters: when he rode, he had no command or direction of his horse, but was carried as if in a balloon.

The key to this extraordinary figure, who talked 'for fame' in an age of great talkers, lay in its disabilities. Johnson was an ambitious and romantic person.

Johnson, however, had a noble ambition floating in his mind, and had, undoubtedly, often speculated on the possibility of his supereminent powers being rewarded in this great and liberal country by the highest honours of the state. Sir William Scott informs me, that upon the death of the late Lord Lichfield, who was Chancellor of the University of Oxford, he said to Johnson, 'What a pity it is, Sir, that you did not follow the profession of the Law. You might have been Lord Chancellor of Great Britain, and attained to the dignity of the peerage; and now that the title of Lichfield, your native city, is extinct, you might have had it.' Johnson, upon this, seemed much agitated; and, in an angry tone, exclaimed, 'Why will you vex me by suggesting this, when it is too late?'

He could never have been Lord Chancellor with his twitches and his fetters, never a great general with his one bad eye, never anything except a literary stylist and famous speaker, using the two members which remained without disease, his tongue and his pen. 'That people should endeavour to excel in conversation,' he said, 'I do not wonder: because in conversation praise is instantly reverberated.'

He wanted to succeed as a man in spite of his afflictions – to have 'bottom' and to sail on his own bottom to success. This was why the little boy turned back to beat his schoolmistress, whose attention had been 'an insult to his manliness'. It was also why he could not bear to be conquered in conversation, which was his only means of excellence. He attached so much importance to victory in talk, that he dreamed about it. 'He related, that he had once in a dream a contest of wit with some other person, and that he was very much mortified by imagining that his opponent had the better of him.' 'There is no arguing with Johnson,' said Goldsmith bitterly, 'for, if his pistol misses fire, he knocks you down with the butt end of it.' If he were flurried by losing, he would turn round like a beast at bay, and argue *ad hominem*.

An essay, written by Mr Deane, a Divine of the Church of England, maintaining the future life of brutes, by an explication of certain parts of the Scriptures, was mentioned, and the doctrine insisted on by a gentleman who seemed fond of curious speculation – Johnson, who did not like to hear anything concerning a future state which was not authorized by the regular canons of orthodoxy, discouraged this talk; and being offended at its continuation, he watched an opportunity to give the gentleman a blow of reprehension. So, when the poor speculatist, with a serious, metaphysical, pensive face, addressed him, 'But, really, Sir, when we see a very sensible dog, we don't know what to think of him,' Johnson, rolling with joy at the thought which beamed in his eye, turned quickly round, and replied, 'True, Sir, and when we see a very foolish *fellow*, we don't know what to think of *him*.' He then rose up, strided to the fire, and stood for some time laughing and exulting.

It was indicative that two of the famous people who detested the old law-giver should have been Goldsmith and Horace Walpole: the first, because he belonged to a more ancient and more subtle race, which *always* argued *ad hominem*, and which did not share the absolute values premised by Johnson; the second, because he was a gentleman, whose attitude to such values was patrician. Johnson was a middle-class, High Church Tory, who had arranged the universe somehow or other in his own mind; and for whom its Creator was a personage in a brigadier wig, who spent his time, as Walpole might have remarked, drinking Fog to the health of Old England. From such premises, the Doctor proceeded to lay down the law with a strong and facile bluntness, which was wrong as often as it was right. But people like Walpole did not share the same deity. 'You know,' said the latter, 'Sir Francis Dashwood used to say that Lord Shrewsbury's Providence was an angry old man in a blue cloak: another person that I knew, believed that Providence was like a mouse, because he is invisible ... It put me in mind of the Dane, who talking of orders to a Frenchman, said "*Notre St Esprit est un éléphant*".' Such lightness about the First Cause precluded too much faith in the argument *ad rem*, and, indeed, precluded faith in all Absolutes – while the great Lexicographer was pre-eminently the kind of John Bull who enjoyed to 'shout and bawl the Absolute across the Hall'.

They generally compared him to savage animals. Tom said that he laughed like a rhinoceros. Goldsmith said that if he were a fish, he would talk like a whale. A Glasgow newspaper compared him seriously, as a compliment, to the same mammal, and so did Hayley. Chesterfield called him a 'respectable Hottentot', Walpole a 'Caliban', Anna Seward an 'old growler' and an 'old elephant'. Boswell told him that he tossed and gored like a bull. Boswell's father called him Ursa Major.

The mention of the wolf had led Johnson to think of other wild beasts; and while Sir Joshua Reynolds and Mr Langton were carrying on a dialogue about something which engaged them earnestly, he, in the midst of it, broke out, 'Pennant tells us of Bears —' (What he added, I have forgotten.) They went on, which he, being dull of hearing, did not perceive, or, if he did, was not willing to break off his talk; so he continued to vociferate his remarks, and *Bear* ('like a word in a catch', as Beauclerk said) was repeatedly heard at intervals, which, coming from him who, by those who did not know him, had been so often assimilated to that ferocious animal, while we who were sitting around could hardly stifle laughter, produced a very ludicrous effect. Silence having ensued, he proceeded: 'We are told, that the black bear is innocent; but I should not like to trust myself with him.' Mr Gibbon muttered, in a low tone of voice, 'I should not like to trust myself with *you*.'

It was true that the most usual simile for him was that of a Bear, and it was only when his acquaintances grew to love him more closely that they realized, like Boswell, 'that he had nothing of the bear about him, but the skin'. The old animal had a tender heart.

Nor would it be just under this head, to omit the fondness which he shewed for animals which he had taken under his protection. I never shall forget the indulgence with which he treated Hodge his cat: for whom he himself used to go out and buy oysters, lest the servants having that trouble should take a dislike to the poor creature. I am, unluckily, one of those who have an antipathy to a cat, so that I am uneasy when in the room with one; and I own, I frequently suffered a good deal from the presence of this same Hodge. I recollect him one day scrambling up Dr Johnson's breast, apparently with much satisfaction, while my friend, smiling, and half whistling, rubbed down his back, and pulled him by the tail; and, when I observed he was a fine cat, saying: 'Why, yes, Sir; but I have had cats whom I liked better than this;' and then, as if perceiving Hodge to be out of countenance, adding, 'but he is a very fine cat, a very fine cat indeed.'

This reminds me of the ludicrous account which he gave Mr Langton, of the despicable state of a young gentleman of good family. 'Sir, when I heard of him last, he was running about town shooting cats.' And then, in a sort of kindly reverie, he bethought himself of his own favourite cat, and said, 'But Hodge shan't be shot: no, no, Hodge shall not be shot.'

His house, when he was rich enough to afford it, was a hospital for poor and afflicted people: for Dr Levett, Mrs Williams, Desmoulins, Miss Carmichael, and for the black servant. He bore no malice for momentary defeats. Sometimes the 'whiff and wind of his fell sword' was terrible enough: but sometimes the blow was held back, the pistol-butt not brought into action, and a blush would actually mantle the awful cheek:

I was at this time myself a water-drinker, upon trial, by Johnson's recommendation. JOHNSON: 'Boswell is a bolder combatant than Sir Joshua: he argues for wine without the help of wine: but Sir Joshua with it.' SIR JOSHUA REYNOLDS: 'But to please one's company is a strong motive.' JOHNSON (who from drinking only water [at that time] supposed everybody who drank wine to be elevated): 'I won't argue any more with you, Sir. You are too far gone.' SIR JOSHUA: 'I should have thought so indeed, Sir, had I made such a speech as you have now done.' JOHNSON (drawing himself in, and I really thought blushing): 'Nay, don't be angry. I did not mean to offend you.'

Sometimes he would apologize even more touchingly, after the stroke:

The Gentleman who had dined with us at Dr Percy's came in. Johnson attacked the Americans with intemperate vehemence of abuse. I said something in their favour; and added that I was always sorry when he talked on that subject. This, it seems, exasperated him, though he said nothing at the time. The cloud was charged with sulphureous vapour, which was afterwards to burst in thunder. – We talked of a gentleman who was running out his fortune in London; and I said, 'We must get him out of it. All his friends must quarrel with him, and that will soon drive him away.' JOHNSON: 'Nay, Sir, we'll send *you* to him. If your company does not drive a man out of his house, nothing will.' This was a horrible shock, for which there was no visible cause. I afterwards asked him, why he had said so harsh a thing. JOHNSON: 'Because, Sir, you made me angry about the Americans.' BOSWELL: 'But why did you not take your revenge directly?' JOHNSON (smiling): 'Because, Sir, I had nothing ready. A man cannot strike till he has weapons.' This was a candid and pleasant confession.

Behind the roars and bumps, there was the pathos of the wretched child which had turned to beat its mistress:

Surely I shall not spend my whole life with my own total disapprobation?

Johnson's *Prayers and Meditations*

On Monday, the 16th, I sat for my picture and walked a considerable way without inconvenience. In the afternoon and evening I felt myself light and easy, and began to plan schemes of life. Thus I went to bed, and in a short time waked and sat up, as has been long my custom, when I felt a confusion and indistinctness in my head, which lasted I suppose about half a minute. I was alarmed, and prayed God, that however he might afflict my body, he would spare my understanding. This prayer, that I might try the integrity of my faculties, I made in Latin verse. The lines were not very good, but I knew them not to be very good: I made them easily, and concluded myself to be unimpared in my faculties.

Soon after I perceived that I had suffered a paralytic stroke, and that my speech was taken from me. I had no pain, and so little dejection in this dreadful state that I wondered at my own apathy, and considered that perhaps death itself when it should come, would excite less horror than seems now to attend it.

In order to rouse the vocal organs, I took two drams. Wine has been celebrated for the production of eloquence. I put myself into violent motion, and I think repeated it; but all was vain. I then went to bed, and strange as it may seem, I think slept. When I saw light, it was time to contrive what I should do. Though God stopped my speech, he left me my hand; I enjoyed a mercy which was not granted to my dear friend Lawrence, who now perhaps overlooks me as I am writing, and rejoices that I have what he wanted. My first note was necessarily to my servant, who came in talking, and could not immediately comprehend why he should read what I put into his hands.

I then wrote a card to Mr Allen, that I might have a discreet friend at hand, to act as occasion should require. In penning this note, I had some difficulty; my hand, I knew not how or why, made wrong letters. I then wrote to Dr Taylor to come to me, and bring Dr Heberden; and I sent to Dr Brocklesby, who is my neighbour. My physicians are very friendly, and give me great hopes; but you may imagine my situation. I have so far recovered my vocal powers as to repeat the Lord's Prayer with no very imperfect articulation.

JOHNSON TO MRS THRALE

In spite of his melancholia, however, it would be idle to think of him as a pathetic character. Cheerfulness, as he remarked, kept breaking in. So did comedy.

'When I was ill,' said he, 'I desired he [Mr Langton] would tell me sincerely in what he thought my life was faulty. Sir, he brought me a sheet of paper, on which he had written down several texts of Scripture, recommending Christian charity. And when I questioned him what occasion I had given for such an animadversion, all that he could say amounted to this, – that I sometimes contradicted people in conversation. Now what harm does it do to any man to be contradicted?' BOSWELL: 'I suppose he meant the *manner* of doing it; roughly and harshly.' JOHNSON: 'And who is the worse for that?' BOSWELL: 'It hurts people of weaker nerves.' JOHNSON: 'I know no such weak-nerved people.' ...

Johnson, at the time when the paper was presented to him, though at first pleased with the attention of his friend, whom he thanked in an earnest manner, soon exclaimed, in a loud and angry tone, 'What is your drift, Sir?' Sir Joshua Reynolds pleasantly observed, that it was a scene for a comedy, to see a penitent get into a violent passion, and belabour his confessor.

There it seems equally pleasant to leave the old Hottentot, angrily rebutting the only failing which could be laid to his charge, and there he died, at the age of seventy-five, after his long reign as the greatest debater in England. The feat by which he had established that claim for ever, was perhaps the *hysteron proteron* with which he had once defeated a Thames bargee, on his own water:

It is well known that there was formerly a rude custom for those who were sailing upon the Thames to accost each other as they passed in the most abusive language they could invent, generally, however, with as much satirical humour as they were capable of producing. Addison gives a specimen of this ribaldry, in number 385 of the 'Spectator', when Sir Roger de Coverly and he are going to Spring Garden. Johnson was once eminently successful in this species of contest; a fellow having attacked him with some coarse raillery, Johnson answered him thus, 'Sir, your wife, *under pretence of keeping a bawdy house*, is a receiver of stolen goods.'

CHAPTER THIRTEEN

Tears

HUMANS have a faculty for believing that their own fashions are right and proper, and that these have been ordained to exist as such since the beginning of time. We have a fashion in the twentieth century of considering tears to be unmanly, so we assume that they have always been effeminate. But there have been periods when it has been correct for males to cry, and when males have cried, loud and long, about a surprising variety of subjects, to the applause and even to the admiration of their friends.

In Chaucer, both sexes weep indiscriminately: Troilus cried, and so did the tedious paladins, Palamon and Arcite. Almost every bruiser in the *Morte d'Arthur* would burst into tears sooner or later, and Lancelot wept 'as he had been a child that had been beaten'. The first lachrymose period seems to have reached without interruption to the days of Shakespeare, when there was a slight swing in the opposite direction. 'Albeit unused to the melting mood', the tragic hero then explained, with a hint of apology, before proceeding to shed his tears as fast as the Arabian tree her medicinable gum. Curiously enough, the reaction against the accepted fashion began on the Continent at about the same time, and Sancho Panza was always boasting that he was not a crying man. There followed a brief Elizabethan or Caroline interlude, when only women and schoolboys who had been whipped were expected to blubber.

It was in the Age of Scandal, however, that a strange

unlikelihood began to appear. The eighteenth century, that unromantic, tea-drinking, Pope-reading, road-middling, classical age: surely we would not have expected such dry old sticks as lived in that to cry? But they howled. More than the most dramatic Elizabethans, publicly, for little or nothing, the duelling gentlemen sobbed their eyes out whenever they could. They wrote proudly to Gray, telling him that they had cried on every page of his *Elegy*. They wailed over the sentimental Sterne. They quarrelled with old friends in the House of Commons, and were led out, in floods of tears, by admiring supporters. 'Prodigious clamours and interruption arose from Mr Fox's friends; but he, though still applauding the French, burst into tears and lamentations on the loss of Burke's friendship, and endeavoured to make atonement, but in vain, though Burke wept too' – Walpole to Miss Berry, 12.5.1791. As late as 1815, Creevey was relating that 'there was not a dry eye in the House ... Tierney sobbed so, he was unable to speak; I never saw a more affecting scene'. They assumed office in the newest Ministry with the same extraordinary emotion. 'On Friday this august remnant of the Pelhams [the Duke of Newcastle] went to court for the first time. At the foot of the stairs he cried and sank down: the yeomen of the guard were forced to drag him up under the arms. When the closet-door opened, he flung himself at his length at the King's feet, sobbed, and cried, "God bless your Majesty! God preserve your Majesty!" and lay there howling and embracing the King's knees, with one foot so extended, that my Lord Coventry, who was *luckily* in waiting, and begged the standers-by to retire, with – "For God's sake, gentlemen, don't look at a great man in distress," endeavouring to shut the door, caught his Grace's foot, and made him roar out with pain' – Walpole to

Bentley, 17.3.1754. (On the same occasion, Selwyn was told that a lady of the Pelham family 'had not shed one tear!' 'And pray,' said Selwyn, 'don't she intend it?') At the theatre, the whole house had to weep if it were a tragedy; it was *de rigueur*; if not, the play was considered to have failed. Fox would go to Drury Lane to pay Mrs Siddons 'the copious tribute of tears' (Wraxall). 'The tears came into my eyes' (on seeing a play called *Aelfrida* being very badly performed at Covent Garden) 'and streamed down the Duchess of Richmond's lovely cheeks' – Walpole to Mason, 19.11.1773. A play by a certain Dr Delap was a failure, but he consoled himself by stating that the leading lady had 'spoilt his Hecuba with sobbing so much, and that she was really so moved that she fell into fits behind the scenes' – Gray to Mason, 17.3.1762.

They cried when they were in love. 'When he was first in love with Lady Hertford', wrote Creevey of his Prinney, 'I have seen tears run down his cheeks at dinner.' They also cried when they had fallen out of love, and were dismissing their mistresses. 'I am just preparing to escort the poor little Tondino to Dover', wrote the old reprobate Queensberry. 'The sound of her voice fills my eyes with fresh tears. My dear George, *j'ai le cœur si serré que je ne suis bon à present qu'à pleurer.*' They cried when their sinecures went wrong. '[The Prince] had just given Sheridan the office of Auditor of the Duchy of Cornwall, worth about £1,200 per annum, and Sheridan was most anxious that the Prince should transfer the appointment to his son, Tom Sheridan, who was just then married. What Sheridan's object in this was, cannot be exactly made out; whether it really was affection for Tom, or whether it was to keep the profit of the office out of reach of his creditors . . . he pursued it with the greatest vehemence; so much so, that I saw him *cry bitterly* one night in making his supplication to the Prince' – Creevey. They had lachrymose highwaymen, who, according to Walpole, cried so much that one could easily have stolen their blunderbusses. Even their executioners were tearful. 'When the rope was put round his neck, he turned pale, but recovered his countenance instantly, and was but seven minutes from leaving the coach, to the signal given for striking the stage. As the machine was new, they were not ready at it: his toes touched it, and he suffered a little, having had time, by their bungling, to raise his cap; but the executioner pulled it down again, and they pulled his legs, so that he was soon out of pain, and quite dead in four minutes. He desired not to be stripped and exposed, and Vaillant promised him, though his clothes must be taken off that his shirt should not. This decency ended with him: the sheriffs fell to eating and drinking on the scaffold, and helped up one of their friends to drink with them, as he was still hanging, which he did for above an hour, and then was conveyed back with the said pomp to Surgeon's Hall, to be dissected. The executioners fought for the rope, and the one who lost it cried' – Walpole to Mann, 7.6.1760. Nor were they in the least ashamed of tears, but proud and jealous of their ability to shed them. According to Lord John Russell, 'Lord Holland used to relate that on some occasion Lord Egremont hearing at a dinner party of the death of a friend, burst into tears and was obliged to leave the room. While everyone pitied him, Mr Crawfurd said testily, "If *I* hear of the death of a friend, *I* burst into tears, and if *I* am overcome, *I* leave the room".'

The jealousy of accomplished weepers came to a head in Fanny Burney, who became positively cattish about an unfortunate girl called Sophy Streatfield, because the latter was able to cry at will. It was because Fanny herself was probably the second-best weeper in the kingdom, and could not endure to be beaten. (The third-best weeper was Anna Seward who, on revisiting her father's rectory in 1793, 'could not restrain the gushing tears, through almost the whole of the five hours I passed in that dear village'.) Large tracts of Fanny's employment at Court were passed in tears, which she recorded with relish. When a harmless mad woman had attempted to stab the King with a blunt table knife, without doing him any harm whatever, 'the Queen glanced round upon the Duchess of Ancaster and Lady Charlotte Bertie, both of whom had burst into tears. "How I envy you!" she exclaimed; "I cannot cry!"' The news was reported in the Palace, and there was not 'a dry eye in either of the Lodges, on the recital of his danger'. At the evening concert, 'the Princesses wept continually. The Queen, still more deeply struck, could only from time to time hold out her hand to the King, and say – "I have you yet!" ... When I went to the Queen at night, she scarce once oped her lips. Indeed, I could not look at her without feeling the tears ready to start into my eyes'.

The real howl came when George went mad. That old horror Thurlow, a Lord Chancellor of even more duplicity than most Lords Chancellor, spoke to the House 'in a state of agitation which continued till a flood of tears came to his relief' – he happened to be lying – and, when allowed to visit the lunatic monarch, he came out 'so extremely affected ... that the tears rolled down his cheeks, and his feet had difficulty to support him'. At Windsor, the Queen glided down a passage 'drowned in tears', and 'the footmen, the housemaids, the porter, the sentinels, all cried, even bitterly, as they looked on'. It was as bad when the

King got better, for his loyal subjects began to celebrate. 'I assure you,' wrote Fanny proudly, 'I cried twenty times in the day.'

This was strange, when one comes to think of it, and unlike what ought to have been expected in an un-Romantic age. It was only when the Romantics themselves came along, that people began to dry their eyes. Here again, it was the opposite of the expected. It was the Romantics who began to frown on masculine emotion. They still wept a good deal, but uneasily, like Othello. By Tennyson's time, people felt shamefaced when they did so. 'Tears, idle tears', they had to explain uncomfortably, before they could let them flow. Unpoetical people even tried to hide them under the bedclothes.

> Oh, would I were dead now,
> Or up in my bed now,
> To cover my head now
>   And have a good cry!

In the end, it was positively asserted, even by the poets, that weeping in males was not to be the thing. They were to work instead. For men must work, stated Charles Kingsley firmly, and women must weep, and the sooner it's over, the sooner to sleep. The fiat had gone forth, under which we labour today.

But will the fashion continue? There have been more sobbing centuries in the past than there have been stoical ones. If this little history of emotion is accurate, then the changes from one fashion to the other have generally happened under a Queen – under Elizabeth, Anne, or Victoria. Are we ourselves, under some future Elizabeth II, to revert to tears? Will Lord Lundy be brought back from governing New South Wales? Will the Commons again be drowned in limpid drops? Will some reader of this small anthology write to its author, as Mrs Thrale wrote to Fanny Burney: 'My eyes red with reading and crying, I stop every moment to kiss the book and to wish it was my Burney [Mr White]'? It is to be hoped so.

CHAPTER FOURTEEN

The Injured Queen

PERHAPS the most dazzling scandal of the eighteenth century, and for that reason the best hushed up, was one which involved a King of Denmark, his physician in ordinary, and a great-aunt of Queen Victoria's. Her name was Caroline Matilda.

She was the youngest sister of George III, the posthumous daughter of Frederick Prince of Wales – though Glenbervie asserted that her real father was Lord Bute– and she was born in 1751.

She was reared [says the *Historical Gallery of Criminal Portraitures* (1823)] in that secluded, domesticated way that it might be supposed the daughter of an opulent and educated country gentleman would be reared, except that she had a greater number of preceptors. As she improved in years and understanding, she became the darling of all her attendants and domestics. That peculiar cast of beauty developed itself which attaches to those females of robust frames, who grow corpulent as they advance in years. So rapid was her growth, that at fourteen years of age her appearance was more than commonly womanly. At *fifteen*, this half-blown rosebud was torn from her mother's arms, and hurried away to a distant land, to be married to a giddy, dissolute, debilitated youth, her first cousin [the King of Denmark]. When she walked to the carriage which waited to convey her to Harwich, the paleness of her cheeks, and her eyes swollen with weeping checked the joyous ebullitions of the spectators.

In her person, Matilda was above middle height, inclining to what the French call *en bon point*; her complexion was the finest imaginable, her face a regular oval. Her tresses were lighter than auburn.

Other authorities stated that her hair was lighter than straw, and one of the complaints made by her new husband, after their first night together, was to exclaim pathetically: '*Elle est si blonde!*'

Christian the VII, her royal husband, was rather diminutive in person, and effeminate, if not insignificant in his features. His complexion was remarkably fair. He had a handsome mouth, fine set of teeth, and a remarkably small and elegantly formed hand. Had not his constitution been shattered by precocious and destructive indulgencies, he might have been an amorous man; as it was, Matilda found him lascivious and imbecile. – This is all that decency permits being said, the rest must be imagined.

It need not be imagined, however, by people who understand French. Cabanès explains the oddities of Matilda's husband:

Christian n'avait cessé de se livrer à une pratique qui, à un âge, peut être considerée comme une fonction de nature et plus tard devient un vice répugnant. La présence même de ses domestiques ne l'empêchait pas de s'y livrer. Ceux qui connaissent l'influence de la 'manuélisation' sur les facultés morales et physiques s'expliqueront aisément qu'elle ne contribua pas peu à peu à accélérer le progrès de son mal. ...

Dans l'intérieur des appartements royaux, on avait d'autres distractions. Le roi trouvait plaisant de se faire battre par son nouveau page de chambre, le comte de Holck, cadet de famille, gai et facétieux, qui jouait bientôt de toute la faveur de Christian VII. Le comte, prenant son rôle au serieux, faisait plus que le simulacre de le frapper; il le battait réellement, et celui qui recevait les coups, accordait, à ce moment, tout ce que son favori lui demandait, soit pour lui, soit pour ses amis. D'autres fois, Sa

Majesté, étendue par terre, représentait un criminel sur la roue; un des courtisans faisait office de bourreau et, avec un rouleau de papier, contrefaisait l'exécution.

The *Tableau de la Cour de Copenhague*, by M. Caillard, adds that although the King was a frequenter of brothels, yet, when he had persuaded a not-unwilling young lady at a masked ball to enter the neighbouring cabinet:

Le tête-à-tête dura une heure et se passa en vaines tentatives d'une part, et en complaisances inutiles de l'autre. La demoiselle, aussi vierge après qu'avant le combat, se retira de très mauvaise humeur.

This tiny and effeminate figure – Horace Walpole said he was so small that he must have been cradled in a nutshell like a fairy – was syphilitic into the bargain, and had been brought up by a drunken father who approved of the birch.

Bien que l'usage des verges fut à peu près aboli, l'enfant dut les subir souvent; il était grondé, rudogé, et cela devant les courtisans, devant ses serviteurs.

As result of all this, Matilda 'saw her youthful charms slighted and contemned by her recreant lord, who, in the company of common prostitutes, revealed the secrets of the marriage bed, and spoke of his blooming bride in terms alike indelicate and untrue. Nor did it end here – for it will be seen [in the sequel] that he tainted her wholesome blood with a loathsome disease.'

The blooming bride's annoyances were not confined to those of the marriage bed. There were social grievances as well, for the old court of Denmark was prudish, feudal, and dull. 'Few of the courtiers dress like gentlemen', she was supposed to have written to her brother the King of England, 'and their ladies appear in the circle inanimate, like the wax-figures in Westminster-abbey.' Also, there stood in the background the traditional bogy of all bad-fairy stories, a stepmother-in-law.

Christian's father, the tipsy King, had married again after the death of Christian's mother, and had sired a second son by the second wife. 'Juliana Maria, Queen Dowager of Denmark, was, when Matilda arrived in Copenhagen, yet in the prime of life, and the ascendancy of her talents had enabled her to form a strong party amongst the Danish nobles and clergy. This ambitious stepmother artfully masked her own eager desire of reigning, under the plausible pretext of regard to the welfare of her son.' The implication is that the Dowager Queen promoted the tragedy which followed, from the start, in order to reign through her own son, the old King's second one, Prince Ferdinand.

However that may be, and it seems unlikely, there was the sixteen-year-old Queen from England, surrounded by stuffy nobles and Lutheran clergy (the waxworks), envied by the vigorous stepmother, despised by her decadent husband, and regretting the happy family atmosphere of the old palace at Kew. In spite of these drawbacks, the fecundity of the Brunswicks triumphed. Matilda found herself with child.

Inexpressible was the mental torture [of the wicked stepmother] when the pregnancy of the young bride was officially announced. As if to complete her dismay, on January 28th, 1768, the thunder of a thousand pieces of ordinance proclaimed the safe delivery of Queen Matilda of a male child.

The imbecility of the worn-out monarch, his corrupted morals, and aversion to his wife, were the real sources of that expensive tour which, a few months after the birth of his son, he made through Holland, Great Britain, France and Germany.

The tour was passed in a 'dazzling whirl of dissipation', the actual expense being about two hundred thousand eighteenth-century pounds. He was fêted at the various courts he visited – George III danced 'The Hempdresser' for two hours, according to Mrs Montagu, at a Court Ball given in his honour and Madame de Vaucluse translated *Hamlet* into French at two days' notice, for his visit to the theatre. He spent his spare time among the adoring populace or strutting in the brothels.

Walpole noted that he had 'the sublime strut of his grandfather, or of a cock-sparrow'. He was 'extremely amorous, but stays so short a time, that the ladies who intend to be undone must not haggle. They must do their business in the twinkling of an *Allemande*, or he will be flown.'

Two important figures had been among the suite which accompanied King Christian. One was Count Holck, the gay and facetious flagellant; the other was the king's doctor, John Frederick Struensee – whose position can hardly have been a sinecure, what with the syphilis, the debauchery, and the insanity upon the horizon. Christian had already taken to aphrodisiacs.

Struensee was the son of a clergyman. He had been born in 1737. He was considered 'a libertine and a freethinker', but he was a good doctor. He did his best to reason with the king, to discourage the aphrodisiacs, to restrain the excesses, and to cure their results. There is no evidence that he was trying to gain control of Christian for interested motives; but, like many good doctors, he did gain control. A protracted battle between himself and Holck ended in the dismissal of the latter, upon their return to Denmark.

Meanwhile,

the fair, forlorn, neglected Matilda, during the absence of her giddy lord, appeared to feel a truly maternal affection for her child and had the infant and nurse to sleep in her apartment. In proportion as the king's physical and intellectual powers decayed, Matilda had made more than commensurate advances. Her person was much increased in height and breadth; her air and appearance, more womanly, dignified, and imposing; her mind seemed to have acquired firmness; and, on their first interview, her enfeebled husband was almost alarmed at the beautiful and commanding aspect of his Queen: reflecting on his own imbecility, he seemed half reluctant, half ashamed to meet her.

Unfortunate victim of the enemies of an unprincipled step mother, and a train of vicious courtiers – at that moment his whole system was tainted! Like the snail that crawls over the blushing nectarine, he defiled his youthful bride. The poison, spreading through her veins, soon displayed its destructive influence.

Struensee was already an expert in treating syphilis, so Christian recommended the doctor to Matilda, as a last gesture before relapsing into imbecility.

This happened in 1769, and the best commentary on what followed may be to state that in 1770 Struensee was created a Councillor and *Maître de requestes*, while in 1771 he had become Prime Minister, a count, and a member of the Order of Matilda. The Queen, like her husband, had fallen under the charm of a successful physician, who had cured her of her malady. Hers had not been a happy married life: she was buxom and nubile; perhaps she threw herself at Struensee's head.

They confined the certifiable monarch to his apartments, and proceeded to behave themselves with the wildest indiscretion. Matilda was nineteen, her doctor thirty-three. He was 'full five feet ten inches high, and very robust; his complexion fair; his eyes blue; his luxuriant hair was flaxen, rather inclined to yellow'. But 'his neck was short, and he was a little in-kneed'. He fenced, danced, and rode well. 'He wore his hair dressed like the Queen, namely, two curls on each side, a high toupee, the hair behind plaited, and made fast with a comb.'

Even at this period [continues the *Historical Gallery*, several pages later] the disposition of Matilda had lost much of that gentleness and good-nature which had distinguished her on her first arrival in Denmark. Her carriage had become more bold and confident; her temper more quick, severe, and imperious. ... Notwithstanding the daily exercise she took, either hunting or riding on horseback, Matilda grew extremely corpulent. ... Matilda had a bosom such as few men could look on without emotion, or women, without envy; and she displayed more of its naked charms than *strict* modesty could approve; and far more than the Danes had witnessed in the preceding queens. ... Matilda was a resolute and fearless horsewoman. It is believed that Struensee first led her to sit across her horse like a man. Perhaps her masculine and indelicate appearance, dressed in *leathern smallclothes*, booted and spurred, riding across a horse, disgraced Matilda in the estimation of the elegant and cultivated of her own sex, more than her undue preference for Struensee. ... That she made a noble figure when mounted on her majestic steed, and dashing through the woods after the chase, her cheeks flushed with ruddy health and violent exercise, may readily be conceded; but when she walked, the charm was dissolved: her abdominal rotundity, and knees that turned, for a male attire, too much inward, spoiled her figure, and gave her an awkward gait. The calves of her legs were of surprising circumference; her ancles large, her foot short and chubby.

There was an economic reason also, which was working with those fatal *leathern smallclothes*, with the abdominal rotundity and the calves of surprising circumference, toward the downfall of the unhappy Queen.

The finances of Denmark were in a tottering state, as those at Versailles were to be two decades later. They had not been helped by the £200,000 spent on the King's tour – a sum which would now be equivalent to two or even to four million. Reform and retrenchment were essential, and Dr Struensee, the new Prime Minister, was something like a genius. His excellence as a doctor and psychiatrist; the things which they called him, such as 'freethinker' and 'corrupted atheist'; everything now points, not to the conventional conclusion that he was a 'finished sensualist' who had seduced an innocent queen, but to the conclusion that he was a statesman and reformer of a high order. He was a radical premier, and that was why there had to be a Tory revolution.

To eighteenth-century Denmark, his reforms must have been astounding. They included: liberty of the press, diminution of public tables, power to arrest noblemen for debt, disbanding the foot-guards (which was a blow against serfdom), foundation of charity schools, abolition of various sinecure revenues, a stamp act, foundling hospitals, limitation of reversionary offices, a reform of the marriage law, abolition of the death penalty for robbery, 'No distinction to be made in christening natural children from those begotten in wedlock', a reform of the law relating to breach-of-promise-of-marriage, and, perhaps most fatal of all, 'a regulation for the diminution of law-suits in the courts of justice'. It has never been safe to interfere with the revenues of lawyers.

Struensee at the same time dismissed the incompetent officers of the crown, and appointed competent ones. He accomplished this in one year, which does not seem a bad record for a sensualist who had to satisfy an amorous Queen.

In any case it was clear to every Tory that the Premier and dictator would have to go. They might have got over the small clothes well enough, leaving Matilda to be a Catherine the Great, if only Struensee had been content to be an Orloff.

While the storm brewed [says the *Historical Record*] Struensee generally breakfasted in the Queen's apartment. ... The royal palace of Hirscholm was the scene of high-wrought sensuality in every shape. Everything was there to inflame the passions, and afford immediate gratification! Night and day were alike devoted to revelry; it was usually two or three o'clock in the morning ere the Queen retired to her bed, and *eleven* before she appeared in her boudoir. The solitary King was served in his own apartment and was considered of little more importance than his dog.

The Queen Dowager, Juliana Maria, now began once more to show herself; her hopes again revived! She saw with secret delight, the embers of discontent glowing in every quarter of the kingdom; and if she could not procure the crown for her son Frederick, now in his nineteenth year, she hoped, by the aid of discontented nobles, and the military, during the life of Christian VII, to attain the sole exercise of sovereign power.

Her intrigue came to a head in 1772, under circumstances of great peril. Juliana, with the assistance of a nobleman called Rantzau, bullied the witless King into signing an instrument for the arrest of Matilda, Struensee, and an underling called Brandt. This instrument was necessary before any arrest could take place, yet all depended upon the King keeping silence. Had he revealed the application for this warrant to Matilda, it would have been equally easy for the latter to bully him into signing a new warrant for the arrest of Juliana – on a charge of treason. He could be bullied into anything, and feared both women equally. However, he held his peace.

On the night of the 16th of January, a grand ball and masquerade was given by the court. Queen Matilda, magnificently dressed, and full of spirits, danced with Count Struensee. The ball was closed by Queen Matilda and Prince Frederick; when the former, attended by Struensee, retired to her apartments for the last time! Struensee must have gone to the Queen's room; for *there* his white bear-skin cloak was found a few hours afterwards; and Matilda must have descended by means of the secret staircase to Struensee's apartment, where the guilty pair had their last *tête-à-tête*, and separated never to meet again – at least in this world!

They had returned to their own beds, and Struensee had read himself to sleep, when the conspirators arrived to make the arrest. The Prime Minister was hurried away at crack of dawn in a hackney coach 'accompanied by officers armed with loaded pistols and drawn swords'. The Queen, surprised *en déshabille* by a posse with lighted tapers and the same drawn swords flashing in the darkness, made a determined effort to reach the King. If she had succeeded, she could probably have reversed the arrest. She was prevented.

Scarcely half dressed, wrapped up in a large roquelaine, looking with a stern indifference on the surrounding officers, Matilda descended to the gate; where a coach and four, surrounded by a strong body of dragoons, were waiting to escort her to Cronenborg castle.

The wicked stepmother had won the game.

It was only too easy to break the sensitive Struensee by torture – by thumb-screws, his page said later. Chained to the wall so that he could scarcely sit or stand, in a dungeon, starved, but with the additional mockery of the use of his own silver chamber-pot, the wretched man confessed that he had been the Queen's lover. She had given birth to a second child since the days of the thousand-gun salute – a girl – and this was declared to be the doctor's.

He and his minion Brandt were hustled out of life with all the circumstances of medieval barbarity. At eleven o'clock in the morning of 28 April they were brought to the scaffold. 'Oh! what a luxury is this fresh breeze!' said Struensee, blinking from his cell. He trembled, rattling his chains, perhaps from the cold, perhaps because he was a man broken by torture, while Brandt was executed before his eyes.

As he sat at the foot of the scaffold waiting his turn to suffer, he saw with unutterable horror streams of blood pour down from the platform above: and so lively were his terrors, that he was unable, without support, to ascend the scaffold. And what a scene awaited him there! Around him lay spread, in horrible disorder, the naked limbs, be-smeared with blood, of a man once dearer to him than his own brother! – In the dust there lay his head, the eyes and mouth distended, and the nerves and muscles yet quivering with expiring life. In a small tub were the bowels, heart, lungs, etc. – and the block on which the wretched Struensee had to lay his head, was yet reeking with warm blood!

But enough of this. They soused the unhappy doctor down in the blood of his predecessor: they chopped off his hand and then his head, with part of his chin by mistake: they disembowelled him and sliced him into four parts: they dragged the carcases to a refuse-heap outside the city: 'and there, for the four quarters of each body, four stout balks had, at equal distances, been inserted in the earth, with a taller pillar in the centre – upon the central post the head was fixed, a large iron spike passing up the neck, to which it was made fast; the right hand, nailed to a piece of board, was fixed below the head; a common cart or wagon wheel was fixed horizontally on the top of each of the four outward balks, to the nave of which a quarter of the body was chained, and in this state left to be devoured by the fowls of the air. The entrails were interred at the foot of each of the two central balks.'

Meanwhile, with King George's sister held incommunicado in a northern fortress, opinion in England was topsy-turvy. Incomprehensible foreigners, with their confounded politics and knavish tricks, were insulting the royal blood. Ought not war to be declared on Denmark? Should the English fleet be sent to bombard Copenhagen – as it was in fact to be sent a generation later? How was the injured Queen to be saved? Fortunately for the international situation, George III was a sensible and not bloodthirsty person, and so was his envoy in Denmark, Sir Robert Murray Keith. By a mixture of firmness and moderation a compromise was reached. A frigate or two, but not the entire fleet, were sent across the North Sea, and Matilda, though divorced *a mensa et toro*, though deprived of the two children whom she loved, was at any rate allowed to sail away alive in an English vessel, to a kind of protective custody in the ancient palace of Zell. The tragedy was complete, and there it might have been allowed to rest.

Not at all. There was an Englishman called Wraxall, who later became a baronet, and whose interests in life were like those of Horace Walpole or of Lord Glenbervie – gossipy interests. Unfortunately, unlike Walpole or Glenbervie, Wraxall was prepared to interfere in the gossip as well as to record it. He was like a slightly fussy figure out of Anthony Hope, a kind of Rudolf Rassendyl. Certainly, considering the fate of Struensee, he was a brave man.

The Danish nobility, now governed by the wicked stepmother, found that they had jumped out of the frying pan into the fire. A faction arose which desired the restoration of Matilda. Wraxall was approached, with all the paraphernalia of a Ruritanian intrigue: he was to contact the injured Queen: he was to carry letters, each of them as dangerous as a stick of dynamite, between her and George III: he was to endeavour to secure a loan from the English King, in order to replace his sister upon her rightful throne.

Wraxall threw himself into the conspiracy with delightful zeal. He posted up and down the continent in disguise and the depth of winter, tumbling into swollen rivers, sleeping at ale-houses under assumed names, presenting himself at garden doors in black masks with dark lanterns. King George was cautious, promising aid to a *fait accompli* – but not otherwise. The exiled Queen was gracious. Wraxall's account of their last meeting has a certain charm.

I set out before eight, at which hour Mantel engaged to meet me. The weather was most tempestuous, accompanied with rain, and such darkness as rendered it difficult to discern any object. When I got to the drawbridge, no valet appeared; and a few moments afterwards, the guard being relieved, passed close to me. Wrapped in my great-coat, I waited, not without considerable anxiety. At length Mantel arrived. He said not a word, but, covering me all over with his large German cloak, and holding an umbrella over our heads, he led me in silence through the arch, into the area of the castle, from whence he conducted me to the queen's library. There he left me, exhorting me to patience, it being uncertain at what hour her majesty could quit her company. The room was lighted up, and the book cases opened. In about thirty minutes the queen entered the apartment. She was elegantly dressed in crimson satin, and either had, or impressed me as having, an air of majesty, mingled with condescension, altogether unlike an ordinary woman of condition. [They talked for two hours.] When ready to leave me, she opened the door, but retained it a minute in her hand, as if willing to protract her stay. She never perhaps looked more engaging than on that night, in that attitude, and in that dress. Her countenance, animated with the prospect of her approaching emancipation from Zell (which was in fact only a refuge and an exile), and anticipating her restoration to the throne of Denmark, was lighted up with smiles; and she appeared to be in the highest health.

In perfect health! Within seven weeks, the unlucky Caroline was dead. All level-headed historians have pointed out with the greatest emphasis that she died from natural causes – 'of a contagious fever' caught from one of the domestics. But consider: she was young and vigorous: she was at the head of a dynastic conspiracy: the wicked stepmother-in-law was a person of strong character: and Wraxall seldom held his tongue.

Whatever the truth, she died almost overnight, at the age of twenty-three; and the sister of George III, Queen of Denmark and Norway, was laid in the vault of the town church at Zell, near the coffin of her unfortunate grandmother Sophia Dorothea, the victim of George I.

Poor, bouncing, fat, and flaxen Brunswick: she provided by no means the last of the scandals connected with the English royal family. The grand scandal of the Duke of Cumberland's valet was still to come. But at any rate she provided a good one, for her few years, and we may perhaps agree that it is odd to find a great-aunt of Queen Victoria's so closely connected with the headsman's axe, with treasons, stratagems, and spoils.

CHAPTER FIFTEEN

Ears

IF their tears were peculiar, perhaps their ears were even more so.

One of the odd things about the human race is that vices are subject to fashion, like clothes. Between the two German wars of the present century the fashionable vice was probably homosexuality. In Victoria's day it was something more like bankruptcy. In Byron's and Horace Walpole's it was certainly incest: in the Caroline period, perhaps infidelity: in Elizabeth's parricide, matricide, or fratricide: in the Middle Ages, apostasy: in the days of Rome, poisoning: and in Greece, perhaps the greatest wickedness may have been pride against the gods. The other vices existed, but these were the ones which at those times caught the public eye.

In the Age of Scandal the eminent *frisson* was incest. Horace Walpole wrote a book about it: Byron was thought to have committed it and so was Franklin: in *Vathek* there was a suppressed chapter concerning it: de Sade of course investigated it: the Blue-stockings spoke of it with bated breath: Shelley wrote a play about it, and a sister of the great Lord Chatham was notorious for this peccadillo.

There does, however, seem to have been a small, peculiar, and subsidiary devil – connected, astonishingly enough, with what one would have thought to be the least sexual of the human organs: the ear.

'Modesty,' observes the *Encyclopaedia Britannica* 'is not innate in man, and its conventional nature is easily seen from a consideration of the different ideas held by different races on this subject. With Mahommedan peoples it is sufficient for a woman to cover her face; the Chinese women would think it extremely indecent to show their artificially compressed feet, and it is even improper to mention them to a woman; in Sumatra and Celebes the wild tribes consider the exposure of the knee immodest; in central Asia the finger tips, and in Samoa the navel are similarly regarded.' In just such a manner, the sexual attention of human beings belonging to any country seems to stray, during the course of centuries, from one part of the body to another – as is shown, incidentally, by the varying emphasis laid on different parts of the body in the cut of our clothes: by bustles, or by false bosoms, or by stuffed shoulders.

A student of the Age of Scandal cannot fail to be impressed by the number of aural anecdotes which are to be found in its letters and memoirs: a form of anecdote which, in the present century, seems seldom or never to be related.

'My Lady Carteret is going to Tunbridge,' wrote Horace Walpole. 'There is a hurry for a son: his only one is gone mad: about a fortnight ago he was at the Duke of Bedford's, and as much in his few senses as ever. At five o'clock in the morning he waked the Duke and Duchess all bloody and with the lappet of his coat held up full of ears: he had been in the stable and cropped all the horses!' 'There was likewise,' said Creevey, 'a person who told M. he had seen Fouché ride full gallop to preside at some celebrated massacre, with a pair of *human ears* stuck one on each side of his hat.' 'Lady Spencer,' recorded Fanny Burney, 'brought with her a collection of silver ears, to serve as trumpets, to help deafness. ... During this came Mr George Caurbridge. The sight of Mrs Vesey, rising with one of her silver ears on ... made me unable to keep my countenance. Mrs Vesey offered him a chair next to Miss E—; but, while she was moving to make way for him, down dropped her ear.' 'At Moyra, in Ireland,' stated the *Gentleman's Magazine*, 'a whole family were murdered, except a servant girl, who escaped by concealing herself under a bed. The murderers were soon after discovered (five in number) in the following manner: – After committing the horrid fact, the villains went off with their booty, leaving a little dog locked up in one of the rooms. From this creature the neighbours cut off the ear, and set him a running; they followed, and he brought them to the house where the villains were sharing the plunder.' The poet Thomson asked a barber whether his razor were sharp, informing him that, if it were not, he 'had as many barber's ears in his parlour at home as any boy had birds' eggs on a string'. Mr Bagenal of Dunleckny, when his neighbour's pigs trespassed upon his flower garden, cut off the pigs' ears and sent them over by a servant – upon which the two gentlemen fought a duel. A surgeon called Cheselden said he had invented a new operation for curing Lady Suffolk's deafness: so she managed to get a condemned felon reprieved from death, that the ear operation might first be tested on him. It turned out, however, that the felon had never been deaf. He was, on the contrary, a cousin of Dr Cheselden's, and, by this ingenious man-oeuvre, he escaped the gallows. Sir Jonah Barrington revelled in ears, and narrated no less than three long anecdotes about them.

In the year 1800, a labourer dwelling near the town of Athy, County Kildare, was walking with his comrade up the banks of the Barrow to the farm of a Mr Richardson, on whose meadows they were employed to mow; each, in the usual Irish way, having his scythe loosely wagging over his shoulder, and lazily lounging close to the bank of the river, they espied a salmon partly hid under the bank. It is the nature of this fish that, when his *head* is concealed, he fancies no one can see his *tail* (there are many wise-acres, besides the salmon, of the same way of thinking). On the present occasion the body of the fish was visible.

'Oh Ned – Ned dear!' said one of the mowers, 'look at that big fellow there: isn't it a pity we ha'nt no spear?'

'May be,' said Ned, 'we could be after piking the lad with the scythe-handle.'

'True for you!' said Dennis: 'the spike of yeer handle is longer nor mine; give the fellow a dig with it at any rate.'

'Ay, will I,' returned the other: 'I'll give the lad a prod he'll never forget anyhow.'

The spike and their sport was all they thought of: but the *blade* of the scythe, which hung over Ned's shoulders, never came into the contemplation of either of them. Ned cautiously looked over the bank: the unconscious salmon lay snug, little imagining the conspiracy that had been formed against his tail.

'Now hit the lad smart!' said Dennis: 'there now – there! rise your fist: now you have the boy! now Ned – success!'

Ned struck at the salmon with all his might and main, and that was not trifling. But whether 'the boy' was piked or not never appeared: for poor Ned, bending his neck as he struck at the salmon, placed the vertebrae in the most convenient position for unfurnishing his shoulders: and his head came tumbling splash into the Barrow, to the utter astonishment of his comrade, who could not conceive *how* it could *drop off* so suddenly. But the next minute he had the consolation of seeing the head attended by *one of his own ears*, which had been most dexterously sliced off by the same blow which beheaded his comrade.

The head and ear rolled down the river in company, and were picked up with extreme horror at the mill-dam, near Mr Richardson's, by one of the miller's men.

'Who the devil does this head belong to?' exclaimed the miller.

'Whoever owned it,' said the man, 'had three ears at any rate.'

My grandfather had conceived a contempt for, and antipathy to, a sturdy *half-mounted* gentleman, one Mr Dennis Bodkin, who, having an independent mind, entertained an equal aversion to the arrogance of my grandfather, and took every possible opportunity of irritating and opposing him.

My grandmother, an O'Brien, was high and proud – steady and sensible; but disposed to be rather violent at times in her contempts and animosities, and entirely agreed with her husband in his detestation of Mr Dennis Bodkin.

On some occasion or other, Mr Dennis had outdone his usual outdoings, and chagrined the squire and his lady most outrageously. A large company dined at my grandfather's, and my grandmother launched out in her abuse of Dennis, concluding her exordium by an hyperbole of hatred expressed, but not at all meant, in these words – 'I wish the fellow's ears were cut off! that might quiet him.'

It passed over as usual: the subject was changed, and all went on comfortably till supper; at which time, when everybody was in full glee, the old butler, Ned Regan (who had drank enough) came in: – joy was in his eye; and whispering something to his mistress which she did not comprehend, he put a large snuff-box into her hand. Fancying it was some whim of her old domestic, she opened the box and shook out its contents: – when, lo! a considerable portion of a pair of bloody ears dropped on the table! – the horror and surprise of the company may be conceived: upon which old Ned exclaimed – 'Sure, my lady, you wished that Dennis Bodkin's ears were cut off: so I told old Gahagan (the game-keeper) and he took a few boys with him, and brought back Dennis Bodkin's ears – and there they are; and I hope you are plazed, my lady!'

We had been in a cafe together [in France[, and were returning to our hotel about ten o'clock at night, when we saw a small assemblage of people collected at the church door in the main street. There were some women amongst them, and they seemed earnestly employed on some business which the total darkness of the night prevented us from seeing. There was in fact no light around save one glimmering lamp in the the porch of the church door, where the people appeared fairly knotted together. There was scarcely any noise made above a sort of buzz, or as it were rather a *suppression* of voices. Mr Wright remained stationary whilst I went across the street to reconnoitre; and after a good deal of peeping over shoulders and under arms I could perceive that the mob was in the act of deliberately cutting off the ears of two powerful-looking Russian soldiers, who were held so fast by many men, that they had not the least capability of resistance. They seemed to bear the application of the blunt knives of their assailants with considerable fortitude, and the women were preparing to complete the *trimming* with scissors; – but one glance was quite enough for me!

The explanation of this peculiar interest was evidently a sadistic one. It was the period of the pillory, in which malefactors had their ears cut off – and sometimes sewed them on again, out of defiance. Any part of the body which could be used for punishment was liable to acquire a morbid charm. Selwyn, an unpleasant person, would twit Wilkes about the probable fate of his ears: an elderly general in Fanny Burney, puffing and blowing, would cry out while reading the newspaper, 'What a fellow is this? I should not be at all surprised if General Burgoyne cut off both his ears!'

Whatever the explanation, it is nice to think that this rather attractive organ, with the delicate pink cartilaginous whorls of helix and antihelix, has had its day of importance. It was so important that they actually went to war about it. A sea-captain whose ear had been amputated by the Spaniards brought it back in a box, and displayed it before the House of Commons, amid scenes of 'the utmost public indignation'. They asked him what his feelings were when he found himself in the hands of such barbarians? 'I committed my soul to God,' he nobly replied, 'and my cause to my country.' So England went to war with Spain in 1739, the War of Jenkins's Ear, and this is probably the only war on record which has taken its name from a part of the human body.

CHAPTER SIXTEEN

Bluebeard

On Whit-tues day [wrote Madame du Deffand to Horace Walpole on 12 April 1768], he encountered a woman, about thirty years old, who asked him for alms. He questioned her at length, expressed his sympathy, and, to relieve her poverty, offered her the post of caretaker at his pleasure house near Paris. The woman agreed to come and report the next day. On her arrival the Marquis showed her every nook and cranny of the house, and finally conducted her to an attic, where he locked the door and commanded her to undress. She threw herself at his feet, and implored him to spare her, as she was a respectable woman. He pulled a pistol from his pocket and ordered her to obey him; which she did forthwith. Then he bound her hands together, and beat her cruelly until the blood flowed. Producing a box of ointment from his coat he rubbed it into the wounds, then went out, leaving her lying on the floor. I do not know whether he gave her food or drink. In any case he did not return until the next day, when he examined her wounds and made certain that the ointment had taken effect. Then he seized a knife and slashed her whole body, smeared the ointment on again, and went away. The poor wretch succeeded in loosening her bonds, and escaped through the window to the street below. It is not known whether she was hurt by the fall. There was a great uproar, and the Lieutenant-General was informed. De Sade was arrested, and, they say, taken to Saumur prison. He made out that he was testing the healing powers of a certain ointment.

Next day, she added further details:

After the ointment had been applied he unbound the

woman, and laid her in a good bed. As soon as she was alone she contrived to escape through the window with the aid of the sheets and the bedspread. The magistrate at Arceuil advised her to lodge a complaint with the Public Prosecutor and the Lieutenant of Police, who had Sade arrested. He gloried in the unheard-of shamelessness of his crime, declaring that it was a noble action, by which he had made known to the world an ointment which would heal all wounds immediately. In this particular case it certainly seems to have worked. The woman withdrew her complaint, apparently on receipt of a sum of money. In the circumstances he will probably escape imprisonment.

Louis-Donatien-François-Aldonze, Marquis and later Comte de Sade, though he never styled himself by the higher title, had been born in 1740, of an ancient and noble line which was descended, ironically enough, from Petrarch's immaculate Laura. He had been educated at the French Eton of the period, had served as a cavalry officer through the Seven Years War, and had been briefly imprisoned for some youthful indiscretion connected with a disgraceful or perhaps with a forbidden publication. His family had decided to settle the young man by marrying him, and they had chosen a daughter of Monsieur de Montreuil, Président de la Cour des Aides, for the patrician alliance. Her name was Renée, and she was twenty years old. But unfortunately she had a younger sister called Louise, who was only thirteen.

The Marquis de Sade had preferred the younger to the older woman, but he had been informed that the elder sister must be married first. Always respectable, with the odd and almost bourgeois respectability of French noblemen, he had submitted to his fate. He had espoused Renée in the presence of the King and Queen, and had consoled himself with a *petite maison* elsewhere –

in which the *affaire* of the ointment took place. Apart from the previous imprisonment, he had not been lucky enough to enjoy the best of reputations, even before, and there had been minor scandals.

'I have strictly charged Brissant,' the police inspector Marais had reported in 1764, 'to supply him with no more girls for his pleasure house.' Brissant was a brothel keeper.

Well, the female of the ointments was hushed up, as Madame du Deffand predicted. She consented to keep her mouth shut in return for a husband and a pension – no bad return, said contemporary opinion, for a mere whipping. The newly wedded Marquis retreated to his castle in Provence with the Marquise – and, after some years, with the additional *agrémen* of her younger sister. The latter became his mistress.

The next excitement was that de Sade paid a visit to a brothel in Marseille, where he administered aphrodisiac pills, containing cantharides, to the young ladies of the house. He also birched them, and made them birch him, and he coupled with them and with his valet. Two of them thought that they were being poisoned by the pills, and resented this, while they all behaved in a scandalous manner which resulted in a crisis. The Marquis was instantly indicted on various charges, including sodomy, and was sentenced to death. He fled from justice, taking his wife's younger sister with him. They separated after some time in Italy, where Louise may or may not have died: de Sade was arrested and imprisoned in a castle at Chambéry in Savoy for five months, but escaped with the aid of his wife. He returned, *sub rosa*, to his castle. In 1774 he was compelled to flee once more, but came back in the same year with a 'young secretary', to the enjoyment of two little girls who had been provided by his considerate spouse. In 1775 there was renewed trouble with the little girls – it was difficult to exhibit their persons before aggrieved parents until the knife marks healed – and also there was trouble with a chambermaid called Nanon. There was a mysterious room at the castle, draped in black, with pornographic pictures. The Marquis was compelled to flee once more. But he was back again in 1776, with a new young secretary who could scarcely read or write, and, towards the end of the year, one of the more exasperated fathers of his domestic staff endeavoured to shoot him with a pistol. This resulted in complicated law-suits, after the French fashion, and de Sade was driven into hiding yet again, by the arrival of six horsemen who had been sent to arrest him.

The year 1777 found him still under sentence of death for the cantharides affair, with new troubles about cooks and chambermaids and little girls in the offing, but with great efforts being made to 'arrange' the complications. He went to Paris in pursuit of these negotiations.

So far, so good. It was in the best tradition of Gilles de Retz, and the archetypal 'sadist' had been living up to his future reputation. But now there began to appear an unfortunate, an even ridiculous rift in the lute. It was the music-hall joke. The Marquis de Sade had a mother-in-law.

Madame la Présidente de Montreuil was a person of strong character and decided opinions. Her elder daughter had been married to a libertine who was decidedly unbalanced: her younger daughter had been debauched by him, a peccadillo which was, in the days of deceased-wife's-sisters, equivalent to incest: but, worst of all, the Marquis was playing ducks-and-drakes with the family *money*. Any amount of incest or knife-slashing would have been preferable to this. The *écus*, the beautiful *livres*, the *rentes* themselves were being dissipated by this exasperating pervert, in hush-money to his various victims, and that no mother-in-law in France could reasonably be expected to suffer. Obviously he would have to be muzzled before it was too late – would have to be locked up, somehow or other, so long as there was no loss of honour, to save the gold. Madame la Présidente set herself down to achieve this object – to rescue, she said, her poor daughter from a situation of imminent danger to life and limb.

The poor daughter, however, was recalcitrant. Far from resenting the whips, the knives, the domestics, the little girls, the aphrodisiacs, the younger sister, and the Chamber of Horrors, Madame la Marquise de Sade, a rather gauche and gangling person with a face not unlike a horse's, had settled down to married life with complacency: she was behaving positively as if she were the owner of a private bordello: she had given birth to three children: she was determined, not only not to allow the Marquis to be arrested on any new charge, not only not to deny him his minor pleasures, but also to reverse the condemnation of Marseille by every means in her power.

From 1777 the Bluebeard sank into the background, eclipsed by the titanic struggle between his wife and his mother-in-law. He was arrested in Paris, transported to Aix, escaped on the way to Vincennes, was re-arrested and consigned to the Bastille. Immured therein, until 1790, he vanished beneath the surface of an incredible correspondence: of *lettres de cachet*, letters to attorneys, money matters, *tracasseries*, intrigues, debts, bribes, manoeuvres, and trouble with the local cure. The horrible old Présidente rode over all, the reins in her hand, and the addlepated wife, struggling on towards the 'great object' of his liberation, besieged every possible quarter with every possible style of letter.

But what was the Marquis doing meanwhile? Always a timid and inefficient sadist – '*Punit-on les pensées?*' he once demanded in a pet – hamstrung by French aristocratic ideas about the honour of his ancient line and particularly about its revenues, he had, even in his palmiest days, preferred to have an excuse, an explanation, an alibi, even in the darkest of his aberrations. Now, safely locked away in the Bastille where there was nobody to slash, a transformation began to come over him. His first imprisonment had been for writing. His tendency had always been in a way experimental – experiments with ointments or with Spanish flies. Now the scientific attitude took possession of him. He commenced author.

A German authority, as indefatigable an author as the Marquis himself, and nearly as devoid of humour, has produced a précis of the first great novel, *Justine*. The extract runs to two chapters, of which the following quotation covers only four paragraphs:

The deeds of Jerome filled the monks with emulation. Justine had good luck once more, and escaped this time to an inn in which travellers were murdered. After every crime the innkeeper's wife supplied her husband with one of the women she kept ready for him. Justine had to entice wayfarers into the Inn, and several met their deaths in this way. Then Bressac appeared on the scene once more – he was a relative of the innkeeper – and took them all to see another relation – a Count, who bled his wives to drink their blood. . . .

Yet another relation, M. de Verneuil, arrived with his son and daughter. He was in the habit of rewarding rich women for their love, but taking it without paying from the poor. He was an intellectual Sadist, and staged an orgy on an ottoman over which hung a picture of God; there were other blasphemies. Madame and Mlle Verneuil were killed. . . .

Justine fled to Lyon, where she met Saint Florin once more. He made a practice of seducing virgins and selling them to slave-dealers. Because she refused to become his assistant, Justine was locked up in a room, and forced to lick his spittle. More orgies. . . .

Next scene: A band of beggars – among them a pederastic Jesuit and a woman given to tribadism, both of whom relate their life-stories. Next: a band of forgers who specialized in hanging women. Their leader, Roland, would allow himself to be hung, and cut down in the nick of time. He threw Justine into a dungeon filled with corpses.

For thirteen years of imprisonment, through multitudinous seas of similar atrocities, but gamboged by them rather than incarnadined, the dauntless nobleman plodded on. '*Je parricidais,*' cried one of his characters, '*j'incestuais, j'assassinais, je prostituais, je sodomais.*' The wild creations of his thoroughgoing Gallic brain violated or submitted to or murdered or were massacred by their fathers, mothers, daughters, sisters, cousins, and aunts. They expired singly or in the mass. There was even an apparatus 'which, in one movement, stabbed, hung and beheaded sixteen persons'.

But the singular thing about all this ridiculous nonsense was that it was unnatural. If there was any fact about real perverts which was indisputable, it was that they were exclusive. Pederasts were uninterested in the opposite sex, masochists were bored by coprophagists, fetichists were out of touch with necrophilists, and sadists were quite unmoved by the warmest ardours of the Lesbian urge. The Marquis de Sade, however, was inspired by them all. Scribbling away in his dungeon of the Bastille, where he was allowed a servant and an excellent cuisine, he swept them all into his net: wrote about them with scientific, with classic, with crazy zeal.

He must have endured countless hours of dedicated and selfless boredom, in order to make his catalogue complete. He was, in fact, the archetypal Freud.

'This,' wrote Mr Geoffrey Gorer of the *Hundred and Twenty Days of Sodom*, 'is not only the first psychopathia sexualis, but by far the most complete ever written, despite the scientific and pseudo-scientific collections of the last fifty years. It includes every range of intellectual, sensual, and physical activity which can possibly be brought into this category. Dr Bloch was undoubtedly justified in claiming for this work a very high place as a scientific document, and claiming that it alone would place de Sade among the very first writers of his century.' Not only Dr Bloch. Mr Gorer himself makes out an excellent case for regarding the Marquis as an ideologist of the school of Marx and as an anthropologist not unworthy of Sir James Frazer. 'The second [note] is an elaborate discussion of the real meaning of the name Peter and the Holy Pun made on that word in which he decides that the Christian Peter is the same as Arnac, Hermes, and Janus of the ancients, all of whom had the gift of opening the gates to some paradise; and he employs Phoenician, Hebrew and Latin etymology to prove that Peter, or Kephas, can mean Opener as well as Rock.' The novels had become text-books, anything but erotic, and the Marquis had to pay the price.

Once – so a legend of the nineteenth century runs – he had been a fine, upstanding man, fair-haired, blue-eyed, having a particularly gentle manner with women.

It was a misleading legend, for a policeman sent to arrest him had addressed him as '*petit homme*', and one of the witnesses for his prosecution at Marseille, described him as 'shorter than his servant, fair-haired, and rather plump'.

Now, what with the confinement and the midnight oil, his eyes were hurting him sadly, his stomach had grown obese, and he was suffering from the occupational diseases of the scholar.

So it would have gone on, presumably, with the intransigent mother-in-law on top, the muddled wife gradually fading into the background, and the first psychiatrist scratching away with a succession of quill pens, if it had not been for the wheel of history. But the wheel turned, the French Revolution broke out, *lettres de cachet* were abolished, political prisoners were liberated, and the Marquis de Sade found himself blinking once more in the common light of day.

As a person who had been persecuted by the old regime – nobody remembered why – he became one of the few patricians whose adherence was acceptable to the new order. He was caressed, fêted, adopted by the Reign of Terror, allowed to pronounce an oration on the murder of Marat. Now would have been the time to put his sadism into practice, to be signally revenged upon the family of his mother-in-law – a *çi-devant* aristocrat – or to try out a few of the mass murders in his own books, and the machines for simultaneous executions, even more spectacular than the guillotine.

On the contrary, the miserable bluebeard, finding the Président de Montreuil standing by his carriage hat in hand, instantly forgave past sharpnesses, assisted his relatives, actually presided at the court which acquitted the Montreuils, refused to set his hand to the more bloodthirsty proscriptions, and was very soon back in prison for ten months, as a protector of *émigrés*. The ties of honour, property, and timidity had triumphed once again.

They let him out. He was old now and as fat as Falstaff. He was living with an elderly tart or actress called Quesnet, who enjoyed eating as much as he did, and he was describing himself as 'Citizen de Sade, man of letters'. The case books of practical psychology continued, to their fatal end.

Napoleon, it is said, suffered from fatty degeneration of the testicles. Whether it was this attraction – another speciality to add to the catalogue – or whether it was the ignoble birth of the Corsican that had annoyed him, the infatuated Marquis now wrote a new scabrous novel, in which Bonaparte figured as d'Orsec, an anagram for 'Corse', and Josephine as Zoloé. It was called *Zoloé et ses deux Acolytes*. The future Emperor knew how to act.

Off went de Sade to prison once again – he had spent nearly half his life there – and thence to a lunatic asylum. Fortunately it was the best kind of madhouse. He was allowed to keep Quesnet with him: there was a theatre in which the lunatics performed, and he was allowed to run it. A fellow prisoner, long afterward, saw him there.

At first I noticed nothing about him but a monstrous obesity, which hindered his movements and hampered a certain grace and elegance still apparent in his appearance and speech. His weary eyes, however, were still clear and brilliant, and every now and then blazed up like the sparks from a dying fire. . . . As I have said, I had only a fleeting impression of him, and remember only that he was polite to the point of servility, kind to the point of unction, and that he spoke respectfully of everything we hold in respect.

He died in 1814, at the age of seventy-four, leaving a will 'written in his sound senses', in which he pleaded that his body should not be dissected. It was to be left in the coffin for forty-eight hours, without screwing down, and then was to be transported to one of his territories near Épernon, where it was to be buried in unconsecrated ground. Acorns were to be planted above it, and, when the roots of these and their attendant thicket had amalgamated with his bones, his name, 'he flattered himself', would vanish from the surface of the earth.

Not at all. They chopped the gross old body up without a qualm: they buried the remains, just like those of anybody else, in the nearest consecrated soil: his name, far from being forgotten, gave a substantive, adjective, and adverb to every civilized language. Nor was this sufficient. An ardent phrenologist dug him up again in the name of Science, examined the skull, and reported gravely that 'the bumps of tenderness and love of children are as prominent as in the head of Héloïse, that model of tenderness and love'. Sainte-Beuve said that he was as great as Byron; Swinburne said that he was greater. Part of one of his novels was reprinted in 1848 as Communist propaganda. Some of his unpublished works are still in the British Museum. They require the presence of the Archbishop of Canterbury, and of two other trustees, before they can be examined by anybody to this very day.

Notes on the Illustrations

Westminster School by Gillray. This is a political cartoon of Fox punishing the Opposition in Parliament (Westminster). Pitt, the victim, cries, 'O pardon me & I'll promise you on my honor that I will Honestly & boldly endeavour to reform ...' Fox replies: 'That's all Twaddle! – so here's for your India Task! there! there! there! & there's for your blocking up the old Women's Windows & making them drink Tea in the dark! there! there! & here's for ... O I've a a a hundred accounts to settle. there! there! there! there! there! there!' In the background a member of the opposition exclaims: 'Pray forgive us this once and we'll do so no more!!!!' Underneath is written:

> Dr Busby settling accounts with Master Billy and his Playmates.
>> Illustrous bums might merit more regard.
>> Ah! Bums too tender for a stroke so hard.
>>> Vide Rolliad.

Taste in High Life by Hogarth. A satire on the fashions of 1742. On the left a pyramid of playing cards, with a bill inscribed: 'Lady Basto, Dr to Jn Pip for cards.' The monkey in a bag wig with a quizzing glass is reading the day's menu. 'Pour Dinner, Cox combs, Ducks Tongues, Rabbits Ears, Fricasey of Snails, Grande d'oeuts [sic] Beurre.' The gentleman with muff who nicely conducts his clouded cane is said to be Lord Portmore, the little black page, Ignatius Sancho. The top left-hand picture shows Monsieur Desnoyer in a ballet, surrounded by 'insects' ('Come, let me flap this bug with gilded wings ...') and the top right-hand one shows various 'exoticks', including a queue and other wigs, muffs, solitaires, petticoats, and French-heeled shoes. The large centre picture shows a classical statue of Venus in stays, high-heeled shoes, and hoop petticoat, while in the background a cupid tries to slim a fat lady and in the foreground another cupid burns fashionable garments. The circular pictures are of a lady in a hooped skirt and of a blind man looking towards her. The fire screen shows a hooped lady squashed into a sedan chair. Don't miss the enormous cup and saucer which are being admired and the prodigious lap-dog on the cushion in right foreground.

John, Lord Hervey (Sporus) by Vanloo, left.
Horace Walpole by Rosalba, centre.
Sir Robert Walpole by Hysing, right.

Gin Lane by Hogarth. Over the door of the public house called the Gin Royal in left foreground: 'Drunk for a Penny, Dead Drunk for Two Pence, Clean Straw for Nothing.' The ballad being sold by the cadaver in right foreground is marked: 'The Downfall of Mdm Gin.' The drunken poxed lady takes snuff and drops her baby. A slothful couple gnaw a bare bone with a dog, while a snail crawls to the woman's shoulder. At S. Gripe's pawnshop, a carpenter pledges his tools, a housewife her cooking things. The tipsy old woman in the wheelbarrow is having one for the road. A mother gives her infant a drink: two charity-girls are toasting each other opposite Kilman the Distiller's where the Mob queues for gin: two drunks fight with crutch and stool: a dancing madman with a bellows has transfixed a naked child with a spit: a barber has hanged himself in a garret: a dead woman is being coffined while her baby weeps, opposite the undertaker's: the houses are falling down: rather a nice dog is feeling sorry for the ballad-seller. Written beneath:

> Gin, cursed Fiend, with Fury fraught,
>   Makes human Race a Prey;
> It enters by a deadly Draught,
>   And steals our Life away.

Virtue and Truth, driv'n to Despair,
   It's Rage compells to fly,
But cherishes, with hellish care,
   Theft, Murder, Perjury.

Damn'd Cup! that on the Vitals preys,
   That liquid Fire contains;
Which Madness to the Heart conveys,
   And rolls it thro' the veins

George Selwyn and his Dog Raton by Reynolds.

Miss Chudleigh in the character of Iphigenia at the Venetian Ambassador's Masquerade. This is not the engraving by J. Cook, mentioned in the text, which showed her with her ravishing smirk.

Admiral Byng by Hudson. He is wearing the great, gold-laced coat which he hurled into the sea off Gibraltar, upon being recalled to England to stand his trial.

Fast Day by Newton. One cleric observes: 'Here's to our old Friend.' To which the other replies: 'You mean the Church I suppose.' Underneath is written:

Fasting and Prayer, attending the Church Bell
That's that's the way, good Christians! to live well!

On 1 March 1793, the King proclaimed 'a public Fast and Humiliation' for 19 April for 'God's Blessing and assistance on our arms and for restoring and perpetuating peace, safety, and prosperity . . .'.

Credulity, Superstition, and Fanaticism by Hogarth. On the chandelier, top left: (upper globe) 'Deserts of New Purgatory'; (lower globe) 'A New and Correct Globe of HELL by Romaine. Lead Lake. Pitch and Tar Rivers. Bottomless Pit. Horrid Zone. Parts Unknown. The Brimstone Ocean. Eternal Damnation Gulf.' The Preacher, dangling puppets of witch and demon, inspired by a cherub whose placard says 'To St Money-trap', is so excited by his own oratory – which has cracked the sounding board – that his wig flies off, showing a Jesuit's tonsure and his gown flies open, showing the actor's harlequin dress. His fervour is measured by a kind of thermometer on right, hanging from a human nose and graded from 'Natl. Tone' up 'W-d's scale of Vociferation' to the 'Bull Roar' of 'Blood, Blood, Blood, Blood'. From the pulpit hang images of Sir Geo. Viliers, Mrs Veal, and (?) Caesar's Ghost. The clergyman's text is 'I speak as a Fool'. His dissenting clerk, whose desk is inscribed 'Continually do cry', looks sidelong at a couple of lustful lovers in the pulpit pew, while the hymn on his desk reads: 'Only Love to us be giv'n, Lord we ask no other Heav'n. Hymn by G. Whitfield page 130.' The congregation nurses images of the Virgin with candles. A female devil whispers in the sleeping ear of one. A Jew with 'Bloody' written on his knife cracks a flea. A charlatan shoeblack spews up rusty nails; his basket, resting on *Demonology* by King James 1st', contains *Whitefield's Journal*. The 'Poor Box' is a mousetrap. In the right foreground another thermometer, resting on Wesley's *Sermons* and *Glanvil on Witches*, rises out of the human brain from Suicide through Lust to Raving Madness. It is surmounted by the figures of two ghosts – the cock-lane ghost with her hammer, and the Tedworth drummer. Outside the window an Infidel Turk smokes philosophically while he watches the goings-on. In the foreground, Mary Tofts gives birth to a litter of rabbits. This woman, a native of Godalming (1701–63), 'declared that she had been frightened by a rabbit while at work in the fields'. She convinced the local apothecary and also a royal surgeon that she had given birth to fifteen rabbits. Another royal surgeon seemed doubtful, and she was finally exposed as a cheat, after much excitement, by Sir Richard Manningham. She was imprisoned in 1740 for receiving stolen goods, after having attracted the attention of Hogarth (twice), Voltaire, William Whiston, Sir Hans Sloane, Pope, the King, and the entire British nation.

Under the engraving is written: 'Believe not every Spirit

but try the spirits whether they are of God: because many false Prophets are gone out into the World. 1 John, Ch. 4, V. 1.'

Dr Johnson by Northcote.

Caroline Matilda by Cotes. 1766.

Le Marquis de Sade. Biberstein sc. 'De la collection de Mr H . . . de Paris'. Probably not an actual portrait.

*Some more Penguins are
described on the
following pages*

MEET YOURSELF AS YOU REALLY ARE

Prince Leopold of Loewenstein and William Gerhardi

382

Your personality is unique – unique in its particular combination of traits common to everybody. This book in no way minimizes your individuality, but it approaches that individuality via widely shared characteristics. A series of searching questions reveals first the general outline, then the details of your own life-pattern. What may seem at first glance to be a maze of questions, instructions, and cross-references soon turns out to be a clear path towards self-revelation.

The authors of this unusual book have worked for many years to perfect the nearest possible approach to an accurate characterology. The first results of their work were embodied in the original edition of *Meet Yourself as You Really Are* in 1936. This new edition, completely rewritten, is a *Meet Yourself* for the present generation. It makes possible serious but enjoyable self-analysis.

NOT FOR SALE IN THE U.S.A.

OSCAR WILDE

H. Montgomery Hyde

1857

On 18 February 1895, four days after the opening of *The Importance of Being Earnest*, the Marquess of Queensberry deposited at the Albemarle Club a card on which was written: 'To Oscar Wilde posing as a somdomite.' This misspelt but calculated challenge sounded the bell for the first round in one of the most bizarre contests ever staged at the Old Bailey.

The prosecution (for criminal libel) of the eccentric Queensberry had to be abandoned by Sir Edward Clarke, and the Crown then took action against Oscar Wilde. At his second trial he was convicted of gross indecency with male persons, and imprisoned for two years with hard labour. He died in Paris, bankrupt, in 1900.

These cases were remarkable for the disgraceful evidence of public jubilation over the verdicts; for the insane antics of Queensberry on behalf of his son, Lord Alfred Douglas, the young poet; and for the absurd vanity of Wilde himself, who tripped fatally during Carson's pitiless cross-examination.

WEEKEND IN DINLOCK

Clancy Sigal

1836

The road to Wigan Pier has changed since Orwell walked down
it in the thirties. Clancy Sigal has suited his exploration of a
Yorkshire mining village to the conditions of today: he went
without condescension but equally without reverence. The
result was amazing – somehow or other this young American
penetrated the suspicious reserve of the most defiantly enclosed
community left in Britain. How he did it and what he found out
comes to life again in the sharp-edged prose of this book, in
which all his experiences in Yorkshire pit villages are compressed into the semi-fictional *Weekend in Dinlock*. The central
thread is an account of a miner-artist called Davie, trying to
break with the pit. But there is much more besides: the miners'
attempts to knock Sigal out with Scotch, the sentimental
songs on Saturday night, and above all the physical reality of
the pit itself.

'He has dug deep into a section of English life, and turned up
with a rich and wonderful book' – Alan Sillitoe in the *Evening
Standard*

'Incredibly sensitive to the mood and atmosphere of this
community' – Keith Waterhouse in the *New Statesman*

NOT FOR SALE IN THE U.S.A.

THE S-MAN

Mark Caine

1833

'Freudian man, Marxian man, organization man, lifeman, gamesman and grey-flannel-suit man – what were they compared to the S-Man? Piglets to a python. In the diabolically clever guise of a self-help manual, *The S-Man* aims a good Swiftian kick at the cult and cultists of success' – *Time*

And how does the S-Man attain his S-Ideal? The first step is simple. He must devour this 'deftly satirical guidebook to success' – *Saturday Review* – in which 'the writing ... glitters with devastating remarks about behaviour which make one start at their precision' – *Queen*. After that, it's only a question of realizing that 'the only overt moral judgement is in the pseudonym itself, with the implication that the S-Man is his brother's killer' – *Time*